WHAT IS A MAN?

IRA JACKSON JR

WHAT IS A MAN?

Copyright © 2021 Ira Jackson Jr

All rights reserved. No part of this book may be reproduced in any form on by an electronic or mechanical means, including information storage and retrieval systems, without permission in writing from the publisher, except by a reviewer who may quote brief passages in a review.

Illustration's copyright © 2021 Roi Arts
Front cover image Design by Michael Chibueze
Author photography by Liam Emmerson

For any enquiries, reviews or requests regarding the book, booking the author to speak or joining the mentoring programme, please contact wiam@pcldn.com via email or www.instagram.com/wiammentoring

Foreword by Ira & Beverley Jackson
Edited by Mickayla Senior
Blurb by Sarudzai Bikwa
Contributions by Allandah & Miah Jackson

Unless otherwise indicated, Scriptures are taken from THE HOLY BIBLE, NEW INTERNATIONAL VERSION ®, NIV ®, Copyright © 1973, 1978, 1984, 2011 by Biblica, Inc.®
Used by permission. All rights reserved worldwide.

ISBN: 9798722192530

WHAT IS A MAN?

FOREWORD

Ira Jackson Jr was born in the garden of England, Kent, in 1997, he is a professional footballer, CEO, Mentor and Business Management and Leadership graduate.

The subject of "What is a Man?" is critical to our society today in the face of challenges for young boys and men such as mental health, economics, politics, social deprivation, and lack of discipline which works against developing a better society.

What is a man is designed to be a manual to advise, guide and empower boys and men to develop character, live on purpose with values that are productive, profitable, and positively contribute to all aspects of life in our homes, schools, universities, businesses and communities.

Throughout his life we have witnessed first-hand the dedication, discipline, focus and ongoing commitment to growing in God, family, career, education, church, friends and mentees. Showing tremendous character, integrity and wisdom beyond his years as a son, brother and friend, regardless of the adversities and challenges he has faced.

This book is a must read and a resource for parents, guardians, siblings, educational providers, religious institutes, youth groups, prisons and community groups.

Ira and Beverley Jackson
Parents

WHAT IS A MAN?

ACKNOWLEDGMENTS

I want to start off by giving all the honour and the glory to God for trusting me to write this book. Some may not recognise the honour and the privilege that comes with being chosen and called by God to bring a certain thing into the earth, but I count myself blessed to be able to bring this book to you. If it had not been for God rescuing me and sitting me down to teach me the truths of my identity in Him and as a man, I definitely wouldn't be here today - by this I don't mean writing the book, I literally wouldn't be alive today!

A special mention must go to the Holy Spirit for His never-ending support, guidance and revelation throughout this journey. He has been a solid rock, who despite my lack of training and preparation to succeed as a man of God, managed to help me to not only find the keys but also to use them.

I would also like to acknowledge my family and close friends, who have been pivotal in the critical analysis and feedback of this book ensuring that the aim is accomplished and lives are changed.

The programme that underpinned this book would not have been possible without my mentees. Every single one of these young men; submitted their lives and growth to my discipleship and trusted the God in me to help them become the man they were called to be. I appreciate them all for listening and applying the information in this book and giving their feedback on how it practically worked for them in their lives. This was extremely helpful in completing this book!

Finally, I would like to thank **YOU**, the **reader**, the **supporter;** for deciding to buy this book. Even if you didn't personally buy it and you got it as a gift - I still want to thank you for making the choice to read this.

WHAT IS A MAN?

When you picked up this book you chose to invest in improving yourself by discovering who you are and what you're called to be!

I truly hope and pray that you enjoy reading this book and that your life is changed because of it!

CONTENTS

INTRODUCTION	1
The Journey	5
SECTION 1: THE DNA	8
SECOND 2: THE BLESSING	16
SECTION 3: THE MANDATE	26
Fruitfulness	29
X Men	38
Subdue It	46
We can Rule the World	57
SECTION 4: PERSONAL DOMINION	67
Places Please	71
The Purpose Experience	78
Order Coming Right Up	87
Patience is a Virtue	95
I've Got the Power	105
SECTION 5: CHARACTER	115
A Flawed Foundation	116
Heart Check	123
The Higher Standard	134
Fix Your Focus	142
Integrity	149
Strength, No Weakness	157
Action Man	165
SECTION 6: THE ROLE CALL	174
Yo, Son	178
Wassup Bruh	185
No New Friends	191
Issa Husband	198
Good Good Father	206

WHAT IS A MAN?

INTRODUCTION

What you are holding now has been birthed out of years of studying the Bible with the Holy Spirit on what a man looks like and how to become that and live it every day.

I have had a burden for the men of God for a very long time. There seems to be a lot of information, consultation, and preparation for the women of God - which is great, but the men seem to be left to do their own thing.

Being a young man of God myself, I noticed that we don't have many conferences, prayer sessions; overall we don't have much men's training. We just get given leadership roles and we get praised and elevated for our gifting's, with no real regard for our character or identity!

This is not to say that conferences are where you get trained, because home should be where you learn manhood. However, as we know, that isn't the reality for a lot of people and, I believe church and society should support the nurturing and affirming of this **true identity**!

In 2020, a year where God had given me the word that this year was going to be my year to *"take action",* He led me to become a mentor. This resulted in me mentoring 10 young men and gave me a phenomenal opportunity to ensure that the next generation of men are well equipped to *"succeed at life as men of God and not as giftings"*.

This blueprint you read now is something that was taught to my mentees from week 1 to week 30 of the *"What is a Man mentoring programme"*!

Many people will be wondering, why I chose the title "What is a Man"; isn't it self-explanatory as all we have to do is check Google and surely that defines what a man is? Right?" You may

WHAT IS A MAN?

also be thinking that your genitals make you a man or the sound of your voice, but it is deeper than that!

If we take Google for example, it is a **search engine.** Search engines provide you with a vast amount of information from a variety of sources. They usually provide conflicting information over many different years, through many different trends of time and interpretations based upon the development of societal norms.

Take for example **GENDER**; what was once known as a world with 2 genders - being male and female, is now a world that according to many has 70+ recognised genders.

Basing your view on society or one of the most reliable search engines in the world to define what a man is, doesn't actually provide you with the solid foundation you need to be the man you were created to be. This is because all these things are run and informed by humans, which means error, opinion and interpretation which causes there to be a lack of consistency.

Therefore, the best place to get the blueprint for **ANYTHING** is from the *Word of God*. The only unchanging source of information we can find to date! Having been written thousands of years ago, the principles are still very alive and relevant to this day and I believe they are going to help shape you to become the man you are called to be.

This book tackles a major problem we not only have in the church but in society also; many men have **no identity**. Most men have never been fathered, some have been fathered but not trained, and some have been trained but not in the correct things. What we are challenging with this book, is the varied interpretations, standards, and misconceptions that we have of what men are supposed to be, do, and look like.

WHAT IS A MAN?

God doesn't want the way you started life, however bad it may be, to be the end point of your life! He wants to give you the answers to win as a man in life!

For too many years we have seen many single mothers, absent fathers, infidelity in the marriage, abuse, disrespect towards women, inability to manage relationships or lack of integrity and underdeveloped character as common things that define men of this age. I strongly believe after my studies that all these things are due to a lack of insight into what a **REAL** man looks like in life.

You may also be wondering what business a young man, aged 24, has writing a book on this topic when he hasn't fully established himself as a man yet, but this is another misconception that this book is going to teach you to avoid - the idea that **"age defines manhood"**!

Many of you when measuring yourself by the standard of the Word that this book presents may be in your 20s, 30s or even older and you don't match up to them, but the beauty is that now with this book you have the answers to grow and improve. You have **the blueprint**!

The Word of God says in **Hosea 4:6 "My people are destroyed for lack of knowledge."** The reason why you don't match up is often because you did not know the standard, or the criteria required. This book is giving you the manual, to constantly analyse yourself and grow in your manhood.

For many of you that have read the bible, think of me as your **Elihu**; a young man sent of God to you (Job), to speak the Word of God over you and challenge you in your current state so that you can get to where God has called you to be.

WHAT IS A MAN?

Do not be someone who spends money on this book but because they are challenged, they do not finish it or apply the information!

Finally, just before you go any further in this book, I would like you to do a few things for yourself, so you can truly receive this book and be **moved to action**:

1. Leave your ego at the door
2. Forget everything the world has taught you about manhood
3. Pray this prayer:

"Lord as I read this book, I pray that my mind is clear to receive the revelation you have in this for me to become a better man, the man that you have called me to be! I am dedicated to putting into practice everything you have for me to learn from this book so that I can glorify you in my life!"

Now that you have done this you have put yourself in a good position to receive every nugget of information and revelation in this book and enhance yourself in life. This book is not to condemn but to show you what God intended for a man to be and allow you to get yourself into alignment with that based upon practical and relevant life examples.

God bless you, and let's begin the journey!

WHAT IS A MAN?

THE JOURNEY!

I must give one more acknowledgment, connecting to this section because had it not been for my mum's wisdom, this chapter would never have appeared in this book. I think it is quite apt as well that it was through her insight and feedback that this chapter was included because she has been such a massive part of my growth and development as a man!

As I stated earlier about us, as men self-allocating masculine attributes to ourselves, this was never a problem for me because I had a mother who realised I didn't behave like every other man. There was something different and distinguished about me and she really nurtured me through my journey of difference by encouraging me to take the journey with God and establish who I was created to be - but also to understand and find out why I was different.

What you are going to find in this book is the journey of your life as a man and what we are going to be helping you in:

1. Understanding your God-given identity (DNA)
2. Understanding the blessing of God over and on your life
3. Understanding the mandate on your life
4. Understanding the process of personal dominion
5. Understanding the character of a man
6. Understanding the roles, a man plays in life

Every one of these elements feeds into the other and takes you along a path to true manhood; a path that for those who are young can be used to prevent many failed relationships, identity issues, toxic traits and insecurities that may have come along in a life absent of purpose or identity. This journey can also cater to the **established man** who may have a wife and kids or a failed marriage or failed parenthood but really wants to make a change to become the man that they were made to be.

WHAT IS A MAN?

As you can see from this journey wherever you may be in life based on societies standards or your age, puts you on a level playing field with every other man, because let's be honest we are all trying our best. No one has all the answers but... oh wait... God does!

The standard you're going to be measuring and analysing your life by is the Word, irrespective of your past or even your present situation or level of knowledge, this book will take you on a journey that gives you all the answers you need.

WHAT IS A MAN?

Set some goals for this book!

When reading about the journey this book is going to take you on, is there anything that sticks out to you in particular? Is there anything you have noticed you might need to work on? Is there any area that you specifically want to work on in your life and achieve in? Use the space below to set some goals of learning that you can review at the end of the book.

WHAT IS A MAN?

SECTION 1: THE DNA OF MAN

"a self-replicating material which is present in nearly all living organisms as the main constituent of chromosomes. It is the carrier of genetic information."
Definition from Oxford Languages

WHAT IS A MAN?

It is always important when starting anything in terms of learning and discovery that we start all the way from the genesis (start) of it. So before we go into detail into **What is a man**, I think it is vital for us to find out **Who is a man**! This will provide us with a great basis to move from. Identity is so key to the building and foundations of your manhood.

"IF YOU DON'T KNOW WHO YOU ARE YOU CAN NEVER KNOW WHERE YOU ARE GOING!"

So, it would be remiss of us to start this journey to manhood without laying down the foundations of identity and DNA.
What makes you, shapes you, defines you? Better still who made you, shaped you and defined you?

That is what we are going to discover in this first chapter. We are going to look at where it all began and what was the intention of God for man when he created us.

The journey of man all started **before** man was even created. It started with God having a conversation with Jesus and the Holy Spirit and deciding that they should create people who reflected them on earth, to rule the earth.

Then God said, "Let us make mankind in our image, in our likeness, so that they may rule over the fish in the sea and the birds in the sky, over the livestock and all the wild animals, and over all the creatures that move along the ground." Genesis 1:26 NIV

Now to some of you this may seem confusing but that is why I am going to break it down for you. The key to this verse is:

"Let us make mankind in our image, in our likeness…"

Now here is where the lesson begins; we have the key text but even in the key text we have a few key words: which are **"us"**,

WHAT IS A MAN?

"image" and "likeness". Let's take this step by step so you can gain a deeper understanding of what this means for you as a man.

The word "us" means the entire Godhead, which means you are made in the **image of God, Jesus and the Holy Spirit** and also in their likeness. The word likeness means **resemblance:** something that you have to understand and accept is that as a Son of God, **"you resemble God, Jesus and the Holy Spirit!"** The way you were made, shaped and formed was to be a **mirror image** of God!

We see this practically lived out when we see Jesus come in the New Testament as a man, he was **fully God and fully man**; because he resembled God physically as the man Jesus, he carried the spirit of God and his soul (mind, will and emotions) was submitted to God.

If we are to look at the Holy Trinity to describe a man, we can simplify it by doing this:

A MAN IS A SPIRIT, HAS A SOUL AND LIVES IN A BODY:

God = Soul (mind, will and emotions)
Jesus = Body
Holy Spirit = Spirit

You were made like God! You have the DNA of God! The original design for your life, way before time, was that you would be a *living, walking reflection of God*.

This new DNA is unlocked upon salvation because you become a new creation when you accept your creator. The clay is in the hands of the potter

> **"DNA is like a computer program but far, far more advanced than any software ever created."**
> **Bill Gates**

WHAT IS A MAN?

and can be moulded into the perfect masterpiece it was created to be! What happens is that through salvation **your genetic predisposition** changes from sinner to saint!

At this point, I think it is important that I offer you the opportunity to give your life to Christ, if you have not done so before. I can tell you from personal experience that it is the best decision you will make in your life and it will definitely give you the opportunity to understand your life and purpose so much better.

It quite simply says in Romans 10:9-10 NIV:

"If you declare with your mouth, "Jesus is Lord," and believe in your heart that God raised him from the dead, you will be saved. For it is with your heart that you believe and are justified, and it is with your mouth that you profess your faith and are saved."

I want you to repeat this prayer with me if this is the decision you want to make:

"Lord Jesus, thank you for the cross and thank you for your life. Because of your love for me and your sacrifice I want to take this opportunity to give you my life. I accept and believe that you died so that I could live, and I want to get to know you more and receive you as the only way to God! Save me today, change me and make me a new creation, I want to experience and live all that you have for me! In your name I pray, Amen!"

Now if you have done this, I just want to say to you **Welcome to the Family,** you don't even know how much heaven is rejoicing right now!

DISCOVERING THE SPIRIT

The acronym across can always help you to keep on track in understanding your identity; you were God breathed and

WHAT IS A MAN?

designed, the flesh you are in doesn't define you, whether that be colour, age, height, weight, whatever it is: you carry the Spirit of God, which is the most powerful thing to ever touch the Earth, inside of you.

As a believer, or **'child of God'**, you can simplify the understanding of who you are even further by this acronym:

S – Spirit of God
E – Embodied in
L – Living
F – Flesh

YOU ARE THE SPIRIT OF GOD EMBODIED IN LIVING FLESH!

Here's context to how **powerful** that Spirit that you possess is:

"Now the earth was formless and empty, darkness was over the surface of the deep, and the Spirit of God was hovering over the waters." Genesis 1:2 NIV

Before the world even started, God did not speak anything into existence until the spirit was moving. This is what excites me about being a son of God; I carry the spirit that activated the voice of God in creating the world! Do you know how amazing that is? Get to know who you are before anything else! You need to understand the context and the content of your identity to walk out what God has for you in your life and be a successful man of God on this earth!

ATTRIBUTES OF THE TRINITY

God	Jesus	Holy Spirit
• Creativity	• Action	• Insight
• Love	• Obedience	• Knowledge
• Compassion	• Commitment	• Discernment
• Vision	• Authority	• Wisdom
• Provision	• Sonship	• Faith

WHAT IS A MAN?

• Protection • Mercy • Voice activation • Grace • Dominion	• Leadership • Discipline • Sacrifice • Intercession • Humility	• Power • Helper • Guide • Comfort

I devised a little chart that helps us to look at the characteristics of the Holy Trinity which you were created with as a child of God! All these things, you can possess and access through a relationship with the Holy Spirit, accepting Jesus as your Lord and Saviour and constantly connecting to God - Your Maker.

This list doesn't have everything, because as you can imagine there are endless factors that describe God, that we are still yet to know but this gives you a picture of what attributes we inherit as you become a son of God. Notice I keep saying son of God because as soon as you get saved, you inherit the new life and God given identity that you didn't have or understand before because you were living without him.

I don't know about you but as soon as I found out these things, everything started to make sense that God has given me everything I need, to play every role that a man plays in life, for example:

- A **son** must be disciplined, wise and obedient
- A **friend** must be committed, helpful
- A **brother** must be sacrificial, protective, an intercessor
- A **husband** must be compassionate, protective, and walk in love
- A **father** must comfort, lead, protect and provide

Something that I really wanted to point out that is very evident in the male culture of today, is that we self-allocate words and attributes that affirm our masculinity. These words form the basis of many false identities of men and toxic masculinity in society which then leads to men being ostracised for behaving

WHAT IS A MAN?

differently! As we can see from the few attributes of the Godhead there are some that might make **"real men"** squirm and feel uncomfortable. If you are going to embrace the true you, you must forget society's definition of man and the fake standards they have set, that change every 6 months.

In your divine nature you possess all these things but in your human nature your mind has been polluted with false information. This book is a mid-course correct for you or even a real introduction into manhood! Read it and receive it, trust me it will change your life!

FOCUS ON ALIGNING YOUR HUMANITY TO YOUR DIVINITY!

This chapter gives us an outline as to who a man is, the context of his creation and the content of his characteristics. Whichever role you are currently in as a man, you are a man first, so your identity is not found in the role that you play but the spirit that lives inside of you and the fact that you were formed in the image and likeness of God - The Trinity.

I pray that this is giving you a great springboard to be able to begin walking out the practicalities that we get into later in this book.

RECAP

1. Society's definition and identity formula for men is warped, constantly changing and will not help you in being a man
2. You were made, formed, and shaped to resemble God
3. Your DNA is of God, which means you possess the characteristics of God, Jesus, and the Holy Spirit
4. Your role in life does not define your identity as a man
5. You must discover who you are before you discover what you are made to do!

WHAT IS A MAN?

Space for reflection

When reading this chapter and reviewing your life is there anything that you have noticed that stands out to you? Is there anything that has helped answer any questions you had about manhood? Use the space below to note anything down that you need to.

SECTION 2:
THE BLESSING

"a person's sanction or support; a beneficial thing for which one can be grateful; God's favour and protection"
Definition from Oxford Languages

WHAT IS A MAN?

In everything we do in this book, we are preparing you to establish what a man is, according to the Word and then breaking down how to practically apply it in your life. Now that you know the DNA you carry as a man of God and that some of you have made the decision to accept Jesus as your Lord and Saviour; you need to know what comes next!

When we travel through time biblically it gives us some great principles and processes to what comes with being "a man of God" or in simple terms **A MAN**!

After the DNA has been discovered the scripture says in Genesis 1:28:

Then God blessed them, and God said to them, "Be fruitful and multiply; fill the earth and subdue it; have dominion over the fish of the sea, over the birds of the air, and over every living thing that moves on the earth."

This scripture has to be broken down bit by bit for it to be understood and applied properly in your life!

As you can see from the title of this chapter we are talking about the blessing of God on man, more specifically though for you "a man"!

So the key part of the verse that we are going to study is the first part:

Key: "Then God blessed them, and God said to them,"

The word blessed in the Hebrew is **"Barak"** which is mentioned 331 times in the bible in over 289 verses according to the KJV but it all starts in the very first chapter of the bible.

WHAT IS A MAN?

DEFINING THE WORD "BLESSED"

1. To be made holy
2. To be consecrated
3. Referring to those who live with God in heaven.
4. To be endowed with divine favour and protection.

Upon salvation you are blessed by God. You have taken on a new image, a new DNA, you have washed away the old and are entering a new. In that new you know you are made like Christ and can walk in those characteristics through the helping of the Holy Spirit. But it doesn't end there, God says **"Now you look like me and are submitted to me, I am going to bless you, I am going to put a blessing on you, I am going to make you holy!"**

Isn't that such a relief? I mean it was for me, when I realised that I couldn't make myself holy, I couldn't consecrate myself, I couldn't get myself favour but that God saw fit through me making a decision for him, that he would bless me. This ***man stuff*** isn't just about being tough and masculine, there is so much more to it that God wants you to know and understand.

YOU ARE BLESSED BY GOD!

I thought it would be helpful for us to look at some examples in the bible of people who saw the blessing of God actively moving in their life, and the people we are going to look at are Daniel and Jesus!

DANIEL

"Now God had brought Daniel into favour and tender love with the prince of the eunuchs." Daniel 1:9 (NIV)

When we look at the life of Daniel there are many occasions where we can see the favour of God in his life, but I wanted to highlight this one specifically because the Word explicitly says

WHAT IS A MAN?

that *"God brought Daniel into favour"*! God did, no one else, but God. Now you are beginning to see, that when you are blessed by God, you begin to inherit the favour of God in your life!

It is important for us to realise here that this is the blessing of God in action in the life of a young man, but why? This is where context is key, let's look at the previous verse:

"But Daniel purposed in his heart that he would not defile himself with the portion of the king's delicacies, nor with the wine which he drank; therefore, he requested of the chief of the eunuchs that he might not defile himself." Daniel 1:8 (NIV)

The favour of God was triggered by Daniel walking in the blessing of God. Remember earlier in this chapter we defined the blessing and a couple of the points were **to be made holy** and **to be consecrated**! What we see here in this verse is that Daniel's decision to walk in the holiness of God regardless of the backlash he could have got, regardless of what the status quo was, this response activated God adding His super to Daniel's natural.

Daniel's motivation was to walk in the blessings and holiness of God by not defiling himself; putting that in modern context, he decided he wasn't going to follow the crowd but instead stick to what he believed in! God saw this and realised that Daniel would need favour with the people in the positions of authority; to be able to stay pure and undefiled whilst staying on the programme, so he **"brought him into favour and goodwill of the prince of eunuchs!"**

We see from Daniel's case study, that when you walk in holiness and the will of God, that God activates the areas of his blessings that you can't do by yourself, causing you to succeed no matter the situation or environment.

WHAT IS A MAN?

JESUS

And suddenly a voice came from heaven, saying, "This is My beloved Son, in whom I am well pleased." Matthew 3:17 (NIV)

As many of you will know, Jesus is: the son of God, the second Adam, the chosen one, fully God and fully man, the redeemer, the lamb that was slain, and all things like that. So you may be wondering *"Why did God need to affirm and confirm him? Surely him being God and God's son is enough confirmation?"*

This is where we get these things wrong, because as we see in Gen 1:28, not only does God bless but he also says **the blessing activates speech!** This speech can come in many forms but in this case it comes in the form of God declaring a blessing over Jesus, after Jesus got baptised.

Just picture it like this, God has created you in His image and likeness, you've got saved and now you've gone to get baptised and the second you come out of the water you hear the voice of God and see God as well! Like... I can't be the only one that is amazed by this. This experience we see here that Jesus has is the complete blessing of God coming together in one! I'm going to break this down for you so that you can see how it all comes together!

a) Jesus was made holy

When He had been baptized, Jesus came up immediately from the water; and behold, the heavens were opened to Him, and [b]He saw the Spirit of God descending like a dove and alighting upon Him. Matt 3:16 (NIV)

For those of us who have been baptised or born again we know that this is the public declaration of our faith. This is the experience that activates us as a new creation and then triggers all of the new creation realities!

WHAT IS A MAN?

Jesus was fully God and fully man but still got baptised as a sign to show us the process of being born again and being made holy by God. It was an action for us to then go and follow that symbolizes the sanctification process, that can only be done through our decision and God's incision.

b) Jesus was consecrated

But Jesus answered and said to him, "Permit it to be so now, for thus it is fitting for us to fulfil all righteousness." Then he allowed Him. Matt 3:15 (NIV)

This is similar to the aspect of being made holy, but the fact that Jesus was willing to submit Himself to John and His life to God through His own will, shows the blessing of God. Through our baptism it gives God the opportunity to do the work in consecrating us. For those who may be struggling with that word, all it means is *sanctifying, devoting and dedicating!* Jesus was sanctified through His baptism!

c) God endowed Him with divine favour and protection.

And suddenly a voice came from heaven, saying, "This is My beloved Son, in whom I am well pleased." Matt 3:17 (NIV)

Now what you are going to notice is that there are four definitions but only 3 examples here in this definition and explanation of Jesus. This is because the final verse that we look at encapsulates both the confirmation that Jesus lived in heaven with God, and that God has given Him divine favour and protection. The blessing upon this final verse is so profound yet so concise it is a beautiful verse!

WHAT IS A MAN?

Not only did God appear to Jesus as he got baptised, but he gave him **the co-sign**, the much coveted **stamp of approval**! These words that God shares, are proof that:

GOD DOESN'T BLESS YOU AND STAY SILENT!

God doesn't just bless without saying something, whether it's a command, confirmation, or conviction, whatever it is he is going to **say something!** You are blessed for a purpose and you have to be able to know God and listen to God long enough to find out exactly what that is **for you,** but we are also going to look at generic purpose of a man in the coming chapters.

Imagine God coming down to earth at your baptism to tell people **YOU ARE HIS BELOVED SON AND HE IS WELL PLEASED WITH YOU!** Now I don't know about you, but I would be gassed, but the thing we have to understand is that this happens when we get saved. God not only blesses us by making us holy or sanctifying us, but He puts a marker on us for the world to see, a hedge around us for a time of trouble and favour stored for us for our time of need!

GOD HAS GOT YOU COVERED!

There is a blessing on your life, over your life and through your life! Through you being blessed by God, people can be blessed by Him too!

WHAT IS A MAN?

RECAP

I know this was a lot to take in at once, but I really wanted you to get the picture of the blessing that is over your life the moment you become a Child of God!

1. God does not bless you without saying something
2. You have access to the full blessings of God when you are born again
3. God brings about favour and protection at the exact point of need
4. Holiness and consecration come through **your decision** and **God's incision**!

WHAT IS A MAN?

Space for reflection

When reading this chapter and reviewing your life is there anything that you have noticed that stands out to you? Is there anything that has helped answer any questions you had about manhood? Use the space below to note anything down that you need to.

WHAT IS A MAN?

Myth #1: MEN ARE TRASH

I know I probably shouldn't laugh but every time I hear this it does make me laugh before it annoys me. The fact that there are people on the earth that believe that men are a waste, useless and are bad for the environment is a deep concept as well as it is an eye opener. I want to dispel the myth that men are trash but I also want to bring accountability to the men as well. You are not trash because the Word says:

"I praise you because I am fearfully and wonderfully made; your works are wonderful; I know that full well." Psalms 139:14 NIV

Now that we have cleared up the biblical reason why you're not trash, I believe it is important for us to explain why you may have been acting trash! We live in a society full of cancel culture and baiting people out on social media and men have fuelled that by not being who they are called to be by God! Does that warrant being called trash? No, but I think the principle behind it shows you how un-trash (if that's a word) or valuable you are as a man!

You are needed, you're valuable, you're important and God created you to play a big part in the world we live in, the reason we hear these cries is because the earth and it's people are crying out for men to take their rightful place. So understand this, it is a myth that men are trash and you can be part of the solution by taking your rightful place in this earth and understanding exactly what you're called to do as a man in this earth.

WHAT IS A MAN?

SECTION 3: THE MANDATE

"an official order or commission to do something. The authority to carry out a policy, regarded as given by the electorate to a party or candidate that wins an election."
Definition from Oxford Languages

WHAT IS A MAN?

I hope that, as you are reading this book, you're starting to get a clearer understanding as to what a man looks like, what is required of him and what makes him who he is. What we have looked at so far are the building blocks, we looked at **identity**; "what went into creating men, who are they, what makes up their DNA" and we also looked at **the blessing;** "what has God given man, what has he said over man, what has he spoken into us".

Now, what we will be looking at in this chapter is the mandate given to man by God, and it is going to be broken down into the different parts so they can be understood as a step by step process to growth in manhood. Like we described earlier in the book… it's a journey!

Many of us have heard the scripture, where it says:

Then God blessed them, and God said to them, "Be fruitful and multiply; fill the earth and subdue it; have dominion over the fish of the sea, over the birds of the air, and over every living thing that moves on the earth." Genesis 1:28 (NIV)

We love to equate fruitful and multiply to just having kids but when I began to study this, there is so much more to it. God doesn't just want us to be fruitful in terms of producing babies, he wants us to be fruitful in everything that we do. For us to truly walk in this fruitfulness as a man of God as we are called to do, we must know what it is.

As I began to study this into more detail, I found that there is a process for all men that they must go through which we see lived out in the scripture Gen 1:28:

GOD BLESSES YOU AND THEN HE MANDATES YOU!

What we see with a mandate is that a mandate is an ***empowerment, enablement, and a command*** from God! So as we go through this chapter and really study these different

WHAT IS A MAN?

mandates, it is important to understand that not only is God telling you to do these things, but he's also enabling you to do them as well. What a loving Father; **"He doesn't give you anything to do that He hasn't equipped you for!"**

WHAT IS A MAN?

FRUITFULNESS

DEFINING FRUITFULNESS

As we've discovered earlier in this chapter this isn't just about getting a wife and popping out babies, this is about a lifestyle of productivity, not discounting the fact that it can be used inside the context of marriage as well. For all the ***Single men matter*** brigade, you are being taught here too so listen up!

In Hebrew, the word fruitful is translated as ***"parah"*** which is pronounced (paw-raw), which means;
- To bear fruit
- To be productive
- To produce many offspring (for those of you who have wives, better take note of this one)
- To be prolific
- To bear results
- To be fertile

Something I need you to understand is that this is not a suggestion from God. Now you know the definition of a mandate, you can understand that this is a serious command but you will also know that God is empowering you to do so as well, giving you everything you need to be fruitful, because ***He gets the glory when you are fruitful!***

You want biblical proof, check out John 15:8;

"This is to my Father's glory, that you bear much fruit, showing yourselves to be my disciples."

That is self-explanatory right? I thought so…

Let's look at a parable that puts this into context and shows you how important it is to God that His sons are fruitful! The passage we are going to look at is Luke 19:11-27 and we are going to

WHAT IS A MAN?

signpost certain key verses that help us to understand *"parah"* in a practical context.

The mandate of fruitfulness is split into 2 key sections, that link to Genesis 1:28:

1. The Empowerment (Blessing)

"So he called ten of his servants and gave them ten minas…" Luke 19:13 (NIV)

The master here is likened to God. God has given each one of us gifts, talents, abilities, resources, time, money, relationships, dreams and He has given them to us freely. He has given them to us as a blessing to our lives so that we can maximize our lives, so we can be productive, so that we can make something of them.

What we see here is God giving us what we need to carry out His purposes for us in our lives. We can look at it as, **"God has given me everything I need to be fruitful, to produce."**

Take stock in your life and really think about what God has blessed you with: how has God empowered you and what are the things you've been given that you may be sitting on and not doing anything with? It says in John 15:8 "the fruitful will be called his disciples," check yourself and see if you've been behaving like a disciple or not.

WHAT DO I HAVE IN MY HANDS THAT I CAN PRODUCE WITH?

It is interesting that God doesn't just stop there, what we see coming next shows us that God is a god of principles and fruitfulness is one of those principles that He has. Yes, He may give you these things and empower you to do, but He also goes one step further and we see this master do it later in verse 13.

WHAT IS A MAN?

2. The Commandment (Saying)

'Put this money to work, 'he said, 'until I come back. 'Luke 19:13 (NIV)

Now this is where it gets interesting because it touches on a few areas of your life without even mentioning them explicitly. When I studied this parable it was interesting to note a few things;

a) God gave an instruction on His investment

God didn't just give you those gifts for the sake of giving you them, He didn't give you the money for you to just have money, He didn't just give you access to a large network of people and resources for you to just have access. God gives an instruction on His investment! The gifts you have been given are **FREE**, but the investment comes with an instruction!

b) Stewardship is a prerequisite to fruitfulness

It is interesting that we see God does not just give us stuff and then leave us to our own devices. God cares about productivity but more importantly he cares about *stewardship*. A real man and a real child of God will also be a good steward and we see that stewardship is a vital part of fruitfulness. Why? Because **"if you're not faithful you can't be fruitful!"** How do I know this? As we go to the end of this passage there is a servant who did nothing and the response of the master is less than favourable, but it is because the root of his lack of fruitfulness was his lack of stewardship over what he had been given!

The scripture even gives us a perfect example of what happens when faithfulness and fruitfulness combine:

"His master replied, 'Well done, good and faithful servant! You have been faithful with a few things; I will put you in charge of

many things. Come and share your master's happiness! '
Matthew 25:21 (NIV)

When you steward the fruit well, you get given more because God can trust you!

FRUITFULNESS IS AS MUCH ABOUT TRUST, AS IT IS ABOUT PRODUCTIVITY!

c) God is going to give you time

One of the keys in this scripture that is often missed is **"until I come back"**, simple yet profound! God enables you to produce by giving you time; a gift that we all share! By giving you time it means He has the right to hold you accountable for how you manage that time and what you produce. He has taken His hands off the resources and the time He's given you and given you complete control to be able to do with it as you wish, with the instruction that **"you need to put it to work until I get back"**!

God is literally coming back *at some point* to check on your results because he cares about productivity and stewardship! How are you managing what God has given you? How are you coping with the instruction on the investment? How are you using the gift of time? Are you maximizing the minutes or are you too focused on trying to figure out when God is going to come back?

FRUITFULNESS IS A PRINCIPLE SO WHETHER YOU ARE A BELIEVER OR NOT, YOU CAN BE FRUITFUL!

Many of you by now will be asking yourself the question; *"Ok, how do I become fruitful?"* and that is a great question. Here are some keys to becoming fruitful.

WHAT IS A MAN?

5 KEYS TO FRUITFULNESS

I. Fruitfulness is a requirement

"He cuts off every branch in me that bears no fruit, while every branch that does bear fruit he prunes so that it will be even more fruitful." John 15:2 (NIV)

God isn't suggesting that you be fruitful, He requires it. You don't just get these gifts, talents, resources and time to waste them. God cares about productivity and so should you! As a tree it is your **job** to bear fruit! Those that don't, get cut off! This isn't a threat, it's a promise!

II. You have what you need

"Jacob said to Joseph, "God Almighty appeared to me at Luz in the land of Canaan, and there he blessed me and said to me, 'I am going to make you fruitful and increase your numbers. I will make you a community of peoples, and I will give this land as an everlasting possession to your descendants after you.'" Genesis 48:3-4 (NIV)

Just like we have read in Genesis 1:28; God is giving you fruitfulness. Everything it takes to be fruitful, you already have and He not only commands it, but he enables and empowers you to do it! God has given you the co-sign and the ability to be fruitful. Many of us are negating our fruitfulness because we have not received and understood that God is the one who empowers us and gives us the materials to make it possible.

III. Get to work

"So he called ten of his servants and gave them ten minas.[a] 'Put this money to work, 'he said, 'until I come back. 'Luke 19:13 (NIV)

WHAT IS A MAN?

No fruitfulness is going to occur if you do not get to work. You can have all of the resources in the world but if you don't put them to work, to use, or trade with them, then you are going to be unfaithful and unfruitful. Assess your life, and see what God has given you that you can *"put to work"*, and then begin to get on it! Don't allow fear to rob you of your fruitfulness!

STOP SITTING DORMANT ON THE THINGS THAT GOD HAS PLACED IN YOUR LIFE!

IV. Be accountable

"He was made king, however, and returned home. Then he sent for the servants to whom he had given the money, in order to find out what they had gained with it. Luke 19:15 (NIV)

From the time you are given the gift, resource, and talent you are going to be assessed on the progress of it. You need to be able to have some tangible results or evidence of your fruitfulness. Every day you need to be measuring the progress of the gifts or more importantly the life you've been given. Ask yourself this question *"Am I closer to where I want to be today than I was yesterday? If so, how?"* also have people that you can go to that will hold you to account before God comes to hold you to account because He could come back at any point.

IF YOU ARE USED TO BEING FAITHFUL THEN WHEN YOU'RE HELD TO ACCOUNT BY GOD, YOU'LL BE FOUND FRUITFUL!

V. Fruitfulness comes from stewardship ownership! (Luke 19:11-27)

Something I've noticed about us as men is that we don't really care for things that we are given for free, (which would explain our lack of stewardship a lot of the time) but when it comes to things that we have paid for, we take care of them.

WHAT IS A MAN?

I believe this is why God taught me the principle of "**stewardship ownership**"! This means that you have been given a thing to steward, like a gift, talent or resources; you didn't have to pay for it or earn it, but you do own it. God is giving you full autonomy to be able to take control of it "*until He gets back*" and it is up to you to not only **manage it** (gift, talent, resources) and then **maximize it** (Be fruitful)!

If you understand that you own your gifts, you will begin to take fruitfulness more seriously and be more intentional with how fruitful you are in every area of your life!

MAKING IT PRACTICAL

Fruitfulness is a principle which means it can apply to even the things that aren't considered *spiritual*, here are some examples of practical everyday fruitfulness:

- Getting results in work, school, sports, or business
- Walking in love and kindness
- Staying faithful to what God has given you
- Having your fleshly desires under submission when they don't walk in accordance with what God has for you
- Walking in joy
- Putting in hours of practice, revision, research
- Understanding that your gifts have been given for you to maximize
- Planting seeds every day in the areas you need to bear fruit in (developing gifts)
- Spending more time with God to build a relationship

WHAT IS A MAN?

RECAP

To be fruitful is to:
a) Relate to your source! **(Having a relationship with God)**
b) Recognise your seed! **(Acknowledging the Gifts inside of you)**
c) Reveal your substance! **(Working the principles of faithfulness to produce fruit)**

WHAT IS A MAN?

Space for reflection

When reading this chapter and reviewing your life is there anything that you have noticed that stands out to you? Is there anything that has helped answer any questions you had about manhood? Use the space below to note anything down that you need to.

WHAT IS A MAN?

X MEN

Having looked at fruitfulness in the previous section, we are now going to look closer at what God said in Genesis 1:28 to be able to understand what comes next. There is a sense of progression in this scripture, there seems to be levels to this, or a journey that the man is going on until he reaches the goal that was mentioned in the creation of man in Genesis 1:

"...rule over the fish in the sea and the birds in the sky, over the livestock and all the wild animals, and over all the creatures that move along the ground." Gen 1:26 NIV

As it is a process, it means that it takes growth and it takes an understanding of the steps to be able to fulfil the mandate of God on your life.

As we begin to look at multiplication, the lens we are looking through is one that is realistic and the priority for most men at every stage of their life. This principle of multiplication goes far beyond having loads of kids and is something that can be put into practice from as young as you like and carried into every area of your life.

Something that is particularly important to understand is that without fruitfulness you cannot multiply. If you haven't learned to be fruitful you won't be able to multiply.

DEFINING MULTIPLICATION

The word multiply translated in the Hebrew is **"rabah"** which is pronounced (raw-baw) which means;

- To be or become great
- To increase greatly
- To grow
- To enlarge or make large

WHAT IS A MAN?

- To become many
- To spread in extent or influence
- To be multiplied
- To have gathered much

Just like with fruitfulness this is not a suggestion but a command and an empowerment from God to his people! To make it simpler for you I'm going to give you the **Ira Jackson Jr definition** of the word multiply, informed by the Word of God;

"Multiplication is the ability to greatly increase what is in your hands!"

Do not be satisfied with being fruitful! Can you now begin to multiply what is in your hands? Can you now begin to build on what's in your hands and make it great?

So, when we look at the scripture of the talents and the minas in Luke 19:11-27, we begin to see a clear distinction between the unfruitful and the multiplier!

As we know in this parable each one of these men was given **one mina each** and told to get to work with that until the master came back, and in this passage, we see 3 young men come back to be held to account. I believe that this parable is so relevant to us today and strategic because it shows us 2 different types of people and 2 different mentalities, people who even were at 2 different stages of their lives.

Person 1 (The Multiplier):

This guy was given 1 mina and managed to trade with it and work with it for him to come back and earn 10 minas. He was the best performer out of all of the young men, not only did he come back with what he was given but 10 in total. He increased greatly on what he was given and then as a result is handed the reign over 10 cities!

WHAT IS A MAN?

For anyone that doesn't believe God rewards you for your work, here is an example of God responding to your works according to the principles He has set! God cares about productivity and encourages multiplication!

"The first one came and said, 'Sir, your mina has earned ten more.' "'Well done, my good servant!' his master replied. 'Because you have been trustworthy in a very small matter, take charge of ten cities.' Luke 19:16-17 (NIV)

Person 2 (Wicked Servant):

I know this may sound harsh, but God isn't interested in you sitting on gifts! Many of us are like this guy, for whatever reason; whether fear, insecurity, or lack of understanding, we are sitting on gifts that God has given us and wants us to multiply. When we see this guy, many people may say **"well he gave the money back, he didn't lose anything!"** But the point of this is that God does not give you anything for you to keep it the same way you got it. God is all about productivity, He's all about progression. This servant allowed his fear of not being perfect to prevent him from trading with the things God had given him. He has been given free money to be able to go and make something with, but his major concern was to not lose it. His fear closed his ears to the instruction of **"put this money to work"**!

"Then another servant came and said, 'Sir, here is your mina; I have kept it laid away in a piece of cloth. I was afraid of you because you are a hard man. You take out what you did not put in and reap what you did not sow.' "His master replied, 'I will judge you by your own words, you wicked servant! You knew, did you, that I am a hard man, taking out what I did not put in, and reaping what I did not sow? Why then didn't you put my money on deposit, so that when I came back, I could have collected it with interest?' Luke 19:20-23 (NIV)

WHAT IS A MAN?

The response of the master tells you everything you need to know about God's view on His principles when it comes to multiplication! He is not expecting you to be perfect but here He even said to the servant *"You could have even just been fruitful and put it in the bank and let it gain interest!"* God isn't disappointed if you don't multiply straight away but He has a problem if you do nothing. God understands that this is a process, so He put this mandate in plan to allow you to see the levels and the growth that He is empowering you to have.

THE PROCESS

When I was studying multiplication is when I was led to read the passage where Jesus fed the 5,000! It is interesting because this is a phenomenal example of multiplication that can help us to understand the principles behind multiplication and apply them to every area of life!

The passage we are looking at is Matthew 14:14-23, but in particular we are going to highlight one verse that stands out and gives insight into what happened before the multiplication:

"And he directed the people to sit down on the grass. Taking the five loaves and the two fish and looking up to heaven, he gave thanks and broke the loaves. Then he gave them to the disciples, and the disciples gave them to the people." Matthew 14:19 (NIV)

The key word that I want us to look at here is **"broke"** because the multiplication couldn't take place *without a breaking.* I'm not sure if you got that... Jesus got the bread and the fish, then he blessed it and then after that he **broke it,** and there is something key in the breaking!

When I began to study this, God showed me that this is a multidimensional breaking, not only is the thing itself being

WHAT IS A MAN?

broken down into parts but there are also things being broken in and over that thing that allow it to increase!

Let me explain it for you, to multiply:

1. God may have to break some things in you

When we looked at the **wicked servant** something needed to be broken in him mentally; fear, apprehension, or assumptions for him to multiply! This may be the case for you as well, there may be some things inside of you that are preventing you from multiplying. What if it's your fear? What if it's your pride? What if it's anxiety? What if it's false expectations? What if it's insecurity? God wants to take those weights from you and break them to allow you to be free to multiply.

You may bear some fruit here and there with these things on you but they are hindering you from experiencing the fullness of multiplication in your life because they don't allow you to think big, think forward or even take risks with God!

GOD WANTS TO BREAK WHAT IS STOPPING YOU FROM MULTIPLYING!

When you submit to the breaking you are trusting that God will help you to bring the increase.

"Cast all your anxiety on him because he cares for you." 1 Peter 5:7 (NIV)

Use this time as an opportunity before you read any further, to really make a list of anything you believe is holding you back. You can even use this as a time to pray, to ask God if there is anything holding you back and ask His help to break you free from them! You don't need to be held captive and bound by the opinions of others, their declarations over you, the fears, and cares of life, you can multiply and with God's help you will!

WHAT IS A MAN?

2. You may have to break what is in your hands

When I say break, please take it in context, I'm not saying if you have a keyboard that you play that you should break it in half. I'm talking about the skills, talents, resources you have; break them down into different parts and improve everything!

God has given you gifts, abilities, life even, and to multiply these things you must break them down into more than one aspect and maximise them. Just being fruitful isn't enough; you have to maximise every single area of your life, every single gift, talent and moment.

Let's take for example, a football player;

They may be fruitful if they train generically as a footballer to get better and that could improve their game as a whole and cause them to produce more. Multiplication, however, would mean that they break their game down into different parts; speed, endurance, passing, shooting, heading etc and begin to work on these aspects in isolation to be fruitful in every single one of those areas. The result of this will cause their entire game to *increase greatly* in performance because of the individual attributes and aspects being improved.

What skills do you have, that you could break down? Begin to develop each one to become productive in all areas! Think about them... maybe even write them at the end of this chapter and then you can begin to put in place the practical steps.

WHAT IS A MAN?

THE HOW!

I. Be submitted to God
- Submit your time to Him
- Submit your gifts to Him
- Submit your life to Him

II. Understand that fruitfulness comes before multiplication
- You can't multiply if you're not first fruitful

III. God can multiply you
- "'I will look on you with favour and make you fruitful and increase your numbers, and I will keep my covenant with you." Leviticus 26:9 (NIV)

IV. Sometimes you must break things for them to multiply
- Whether that is information,
- Whether that is scripture,
- Whether that is gifts
- It must be broken down into parts

V. Take each part seriously
- Every part of your life can be fruitful
- When there are many fruitful parts there is a multiplied life

RECAP

To multiply is to:
- To understand the blessing
- To submit to being broken
- To commit to fruitfulness

WHAT IS A MAN?

Space for reflection

When reading this chapter and reviewing your life is there anything that you have noticed that stands out to you? Is there anything that has helped answer any questions you had about manhood? Use the space below to note anything down that you need to.

_____
_____
_____
_____
_____
_____
_____
_____
_____
_____
_____
_____
_____
_____
_____
_____
_____
_____
_____
_____
_____
_____
_____
_____
_____
_____
_____
_____
_____

WHAT IS A MAN?

SUBDUE IT

We've learned to be fruitful and now we've just learned about multiplication... so what comes next?

What comes next is a word that may not be familiar to you all, because it isn't commonly used in popular culture, but that word is **subdue!**

This is the next step in the process of the mandate of God for a man: **"fill the earth and subdue it"**

What we're going to do here is to split this chapter into the 2 aspects that are the keys:
- Fill the earth
- Subdue it

FILL THE EARTH

Fill: male (maw-lay)

- To consecrate
- To replenish
- To be armed
- To accomplish
- Fullness
- Abundance

How does this apply to us; how do we fill the earth? This can take many forms practically, but the main one I want to look at is making sure that your impact and faith are known across the earth. Through your handprint on this earth you want to ensure that God's handprint is the print that the world sees. How can you impact more people? How can you show God to more people? How can you accomplish?

WHAT IS A MAN?

Here are a few keys to filling the earth, that link to everything that we have looked at so far:

1. **Know who you are** – Once we know the identity God has given us, we set the foundations better to begin to fill the earth. We are joint heirs with Christ and we are made in the reflection of God! *Who you are is the first step in defining what you can achieve!*
2. **Claim the blessing of God** – God has given you His blessing, God has placed His blessings and favour on you, so you must claim that before you go into this world and begin to accomplish! *An untapped blessing is like a free gift that you never claim!*
3. **Receive the empowerment of God to produce** – God wants you to accomplish, that's why He sets the mandate. You can know that you've been blessed but if you don't receive the fact that God has given you everything you need to succeed and be abundant, then you will not produce what God has called you to do. *Allow the empowerment of God to move you to action!*
4. **Begin to multiply** – The earth needs to begin to see our levels of increase before they can fill the earth. You have to be multiplying with what you have so that you are on the way to abundance. *Increase comes before abundance!*

All these keys contribute to us living that John 10:10 life that we are called to live:

"The thief comes only to steal and kill and destroy; I have come that they may have life and have it to the full." John 10:10 (NIV)

These four things we have seen here provide us with not only the platform, but the momentum to be able to go on and fill the earth. Through our productivity and reflection of God we begin to attract others. The natural attraction of success and productivity provides a beautiful space for us to be the vessel that God has called us to be and put our mark on the earth.

WHAT IS A MAN?

This is one way to look at filling the earth; from the perspective of ensuring that through you, the God colours are displayed across the earth; whether that be by you becoming a global success in your career, missionary work, or it could even be becoming someone who is a key decision maker that can create change in policies that redirect the legislation to Christ's principles. There are so many ways that you can fill the earth with God!

The most important way to fill the earth however, is to **fill the Earth with believers!** I believe that through the first perspective you are in more of a position of credibility to complete this complete divine mission of filling the Earth with believers as it says in the Great Commission! Through you knowing God and the blessings that come with being His child, you are able to witness to others who don't currently believe, and when they see your life they will be drawn to wanting to know more about Christ.

GOD DOESN'T WANT THE GOSPEL TO BE LIMITED TO YOUR LOCALITY!

There is a phrase that I heard one time in a comedy show where the main character was talking about when he gets angry and is ready to fight; he says that he starts to say stupid things like *"Anyone can get it!"* And when I heard that as you can imagine I found it quite funny because of how random but accurate it was in explaining his feelings at the time. Then the Holy Spirit began to whisper to me and say, *"What if we became this bold with the Great Commission?"* I began to think about it, what is the premise behind this phrase?

The premise is that the character had got to a point where he no longer cared, anyone could *catch these hands* and get fought! So, us as believers we need to have the mentality that anyone

WHAT IS A MAN?

can get the Word of God! Anyone can get the truth! If we can do this, we can fill the earth which is our God given duty!

"Therefore, go and make disciples of all nations, baptizing them in the name of the Father and of the Son and of the Holy Spirit, and teaching them to obey everything I have commanded you. And surely, I am with you always, to the very end of the age."" **Matthew 28:19-20 (NIV)**

SUBDUE

Many people may be thrown off guard by a word like subdue because it isn't commonly used by people today and it sounds so aggressive when it's said, almost like an oppressive word! This is why it is important to get a definition so you're able to see context of the word, and also make connections to words and examples that can help you to apply this as best as possible.

DEFINING SUBDUING

Subdue: kabash (maw-lay)

- To conquer by force
- To overpower
- To destroy the force
- To render submissive
- To overcome by persuasion
- To reduce to tenderness
- To make mellow
- To reduce the intensity or degree of

As you may realise now; I like to get multiple perspectives on a word so that I can present it to you in the best way for you to grow as a man. So here again we have the ***Ira Jackson Jr definition*** of the word subdue and what it means for you as a man from a biblical lens:

WHAT IS A MAN?

"Subjection is the process of preparing to conquer the world, by first conquering yourself!"

Let us just look at a couple of scriptures that deal with subjection, so we can begin to get an understanding of how this looks practically as men.

CONQUER SELF

"No, I strike a blow to my body and make it my slave so that after I have preached to others, I myself will not be disqualified for the prize." 1 Corinthians 9:27 NIV

Now before we get into the details and particulars of this, I want to make it clear like I did in the previous verses that as a believer you are a new creation but you also must match your humanity to your divinity. So when I say conquer self, I am referring to the humanity, it's being subdued so that it is aligned to your divinity. Your body is an instrument of God, your life is a reflection of God so it has to be aligned!

This version of self is referring to:

Sin Nature
Engrained In
Living
Flesh

Just because you get saved doesn't mean your habits immediately respond and this is something we have to grasp.

In this passage from verse 24-27, Paul is talking about self-discipline and I believe this is very vital for us as men because let's be honest, we can be so lawless and ill-disciplined in the way we behave. We almost walk with the air of ***"I'm a man, I can do what I want"*** but what Paul is explaining here is that in order

WHAT IS A MAN?

for you to walk out the life you are called to, and to run the race you're supposed to run with God, you need to bring your body under subjection.

CONQUER YOUR HUMANITY FOR THE SAKE OF HUMANITY!

What we see here from Paul is a quick look at making sure you have your house in order before you start going to declare to everyone else that they need to fix up. As men we cannot be declaring righteousness that we don't live, promoting a purity that we do not possess, and we cannot be judging by a standard we don't adhere to.

Paul is talking about becoming so ruthless with the body, the flesh, or the humanity, that it becomes your slave. The word slave links to subjection because you must have your body under **control**. The once *"natural urges"* need to be submitted and subdued. I know this may sound drastic but the end of this verse is what brings a lot of context to why it is important to conquer self before going to try and conquer the world.

"...so that after I have preached to others, I myself will not be disqualified for the prize." 1 Corinthians 9:27 NIV

In order for us to be great, or to fulfil what God has called us to do we need to get our *humanity under submission!*

As a man this can mean so many different things, so let me give you some examples of how you can win in life by first winning over your humanity:

- You need to put laziness under submission
- You need to put fear under submission
- You need to put lust under submission
- You need to put anger under submission
- You need to put insecurity under submission
- You need to put manipulation under submission

WHAT IS A MAN?

- You need to put deceit under submission
- You need to put pride under submission
- You need to put your weight under submission
- You need to put your motives under submission

As you can see here from this list, there are a few things that you can actively do to conquer your humanity, through the Word of God. The Word is the only thing that allows you to build your spirit to such a point where the flesh begins to subside, because there is not room for it to inform your decisions or your actions.

You are called to be great and do great things but it all starts with you. God is a god of momentum and he wants you to be able to overcome the world in you before you conquer the world around you.

TAKING ON THE BIG GUNS

It is so easy for us to live in our humanity; the world informs it, society affirms it, our environments influence it, but we have to conquer it. Once we have done so we get to the bigger picture and mandate that God has for us as men which is to **"subdue the earth"**!

The reason why this is called taking on the big guns, is because many people will see this mandate and be like *"Subdue the earth? Isn't that a bit much? Like how is that possible?"* Well don't you worry too much because we thank God for this book giving you the practical answers as to how to do that.

WHAT IS A MAN?

1. The Earth is the world!

"in which you used to live when you followed the ways of this world and of the ruler of the kingdom of the air, the spirit who is now at work in those who are disobedient." Ephesians 2:2 NIV

The world is the enemy's playground, where his agenda is in operation. This is why I believe we frequently hear the phrase in Christian circles **"be in the world but not of the world!"** Just because we live here doesn't mean we need to be informed by everything that the world presents to us. The earth was created by God but is currently being polluted by the enemy.

2. This battle is spiritual!

"For our struggle is not against flesh and blood, but against the rulers, against the authorities, against the powers of this dark world and against the spiritual forces of evil in the heavenly realms." Ephesians 6:12 NIV

We know the earth is being polluted by the enemy so we need to ensure that we subdue the source, rather than what we see in front of our eyes. This scripture gives us an understanding of what we are dealing with; **"there is always more than meets the eye"** if it's a plot of the enemy it needs to be dealt with in the spiritual realm. The spiritual forces of evil need to be subdued by the spirit of God and that is what we carry! Whether you like it or not, this is a battle and one that we have won. All we need to do is turn up and ensure that we are not perpetuating the darkness with our lifestyle like Paul said earlier. Just like Jesus in 1 John 3:8 we are called to **destroy the works/ force of the enemy** present on the earth.

WHAT IS A MAN?

3. Be of a Different Spirit!

"Jesus knew their thoughts and said to them, "Every kingdom divided against itself will be ruined, and every city or household divided against itself will not stand. If Satan drives out Satan, he is divided against himself. How then can his kingdom stand?" Matthew 12:25-26 NIV

YOU CANNOT BE OF THE WORLD'S SPIRIT AND SUBDUE IT!

I love the way that Jesus reacts to these people when they accuse him of being part of the devil's clique and casting out demons. He's really like "Wait are you silly, why would I kill someone from my own camp?" As DJ Khaled would say this is a ***major key alert;*** Jesus gives us the key to subduing this earth and the enemy's work, we must be of a **different spirit**!

If what we are fighting is the Spirit of the world then it means we need to be fighting with the Spirit of God. We need to be walking in the authority of God! The blessing of God needs to be in operation in your life to be able to subdue the earth, the spirit of the world and the darkness of this world! You have a responsibility to rise up with the spirit of God! As a man of God, you should rise up in power, authority, boldness but more importantly rise up in wisdom! You can't be wise if you are trying to subdue the earth whilst looking like the earth! BE OF A DIFFERENT SPIRIT!

THE HOW

1. Be submitted to God
2. Be disciplined, committed and persistent to righteousness
3. Understand the spirit of this world is not your friend (Romans 12:2)
4. Understand God has given you the power and authority to overcome

WHAT IS A MAN?

RECAP

1) **Filling the earth comes in two forms**
A) Bringing more of God to the earth through your impact and influence
B) Bring more people to Christ and filling the Earth with believers
2) **Subduing starts with yourself**
A) Align your humanity with your divinity
B) Conquer your humanity for the sake of humanity
3) **Subdue to the earth**
A) The Earth is the world and the enemy's agenda
B) The battle to subdue is spiritual
C) You must be of a different spirit to what you plan to subdue

WHAT IS A MAN?

Space for reflection

When reading this chapter and reviewing your life is there anything that you have noticed that stands out to you? Is there anything that has helped answer any questions you had about manhood? Use the space below to note anything down that you need to.

WHAT IS A MAN?

WE CAN RULE THE WORLD

The next and final level of the mandate of man, that we are going to look at is dominion. Yes, I said it dominion! That robust and strong word! Some of you "men's men" are now thinking to yourself *"see this is the sort of stuff I signed up for, this is better!"* Well, yes this is just as much for you as everything else is, so make sure you take it in.

We know that God is a god of progression and that He wants us to win and to rule. Everything that you have heard up until this point has been leading to the reason why you were created in the first place. For those of you that have forgotten, remember when God had the conversation with the Holy Spirit and Jesus to discuss your creation, He gave a reason why. Ok, let's look at Genesis 1:26 to remind you:

"Then God said, "Let us make mankind in our image, in our likeness, so that they may rule over the fish in the sea and the birds in the sky, over the livestock and all the wild animals, and over all the creatures that move along the ground.""" Genesis 1:26 NIV

The whole reason you were created was to be God on earth! Part of that mandate is to *rule the earth.* Not only does God give this reason for creation in verse 26 but He later breaks it down into the mandate process that we have seen and been studying so far in verse 28, which talks about us being fruitful, multiplying, filling the earth and subduing it and then now we come to *having dominion!*

If we want to rule the earth, we have to be walking these things out in our lives. We have to be going through this process in order to end up fulfilling the mandate of God on our lives!

The question we then have to ask ourselves is, what is dominion and what does that look like for me as a man? Or if you're a

WHAT IS A MAN?

mother teaching this to your son; what does this look like practically for him living on the earth in these times! Everything that we look at here, everything we study; just because it was written thousands of years ago doesn't mean it doesn't apply to your life today! The most amazing thing about the Word is that the principles are timeless!

DEFINING DOMINION

In Hebrew, the word for dominion is **radah** which is pronounced **(raw-daw)** and here are some of the definitions of what the word means!

- To rule
- To dominate
- To tread down
- To subjugate
- To cause to dominate
- Sovereignty
- Control
- Territory of sovereign or government

Isn't it interesting that these words are very active and powerful? Like God doesn't want you to just be here on earth, He wants you to take over the Earth! He wants the kingdom of heaven established on earth and that isn't going to happen with a laissez-faire mentality!

So far what we've seen from scripture, God is taking us through stages.

1. First, we need to be producing **(fruitful)**
2. Then we need to increase greatly **(multiply)**
3. Then we have to put the earth under subjection **(subdue)**
4. And now God is calling us to rule this earth **(dominion)**

WHAT IS A MAN?

What does that look like as a man?

As a man of God you are called to be a joint heir with Christ; which means you are a prince, you are made and mandated to rule over this earth. You have divine rights to dominate this earth but if you don't know that, you will never be in the position when you're going to ever walk in that. If you don't know your identity, the mandate, and if you're not walking in it, then you are never going to rule like you're supposed to!

"Now if we are children, then we are heirs—heirs of God and co-heirs with Christ, if indeed we share in his sufferings in order that we may also share in his glory." Romans 8:17 NIV

As dominion is the final part of the process of what you are called to do on this earth as a man, then we have to understand that it is a *"product of fruitfulness, multiplication and subduing"*. Every single stage that leads to dominion contributes to you fulfilling your mandate on earth to rule! God has placed you on this earth to **RULE**!

You are not called to be a by-stander, allowing life to dictate to you what you can and can't achieve. You are called to take control of your life and destiny. You are not here to get along and go with the flow, as a man of God you can't have a laissez-faire attitude to life and progress. The earth is your territory and it was created to respond to your voice.

There are things that when the spirit of God urges us to declare, that have to come to pass and respond because we have dominion over the earth.

I'm sure you're going to want proof of this, there is no better place to look than the Word!

WHAT IS A MAN?

Here are some examples and confirmations of your mandated dominion:

"You made them rulers over the works of your hands; you put everything under their feet: all flocks and herds, and the animals of the wild, the birds in the sky, and the fish in the sea, all that swim the paths of the seas." Psalms 8:6-8 NIV

"Your kingdom is an everlasting kingdom, and your dominion endures through all generations. The Lord is trustworthy in all he promises and faithful in all he does." Psalms 145:13 NIV

"How great are his signs, how mighty his wonders! His kingdom is an eternal kingdom; his dominion endures from generation to generation." Daniel 4:3 NIV

"I have given you authority to trample on snakes and scorpions and to overcome all the power of the enemy; nothing will harm you." Luke 10:19 NIV

What we can see here, in scripture, not only does God call you to have dominion but He also gives us dominion when we are walking in alignment with His will and His Word. He reminds us of our authority that we carry over this earth and the things of the earth.

The scripture talks about having *"**dominion over the earth**",* so the question would be, why do believers talk so much about heaven? Why do we focus our attention on heaven and leaving things for the heavenly realm? We make statements like *"**My wealth and prosperity are in heaven!**"* But what about earth? God called you to live on earth, to rule earth, to have dominion over earth! God called you to establish a new order on earth! Heaven can wait because it is not your current mandate! Do not waste your years on earth, letting time pass you by without having dominion and fulfilling your mandate! Our job, responsibility and purpose is to bring heaven to earth!

WHAT IS A MAN?

I want to show you a practical example in the bible, where Daniel shows us this mandate process in action:

1. **Fruitfulness**: In order to get into the training programme they had to display a productivity that gave them the qualifications to be accepted.

"young men without any physical defect, handsome, showing aptitude for every kind of learning, well informed, quick to understand, and qualified to serve in the king's palace. He was to teach them the language and literature of the Babylonians." Daniel 1:4 NIV

2. **Multiplication:** God increased Daniel greatly because of his decision to stay submitted to His principles and not defile himself!

"But Daniel resolved not to defile himself with the royal food and wine, and he asked the chief official for permission not to defile himself this way. Now God had caused the official to show favour and compassion to Daniel," Daniel 1:8-9 NIV

3. **Subdue:** Subduing themselves to purity led them to the position where they were able to subdue others as the guard changed the nutritional plan to match that of Daniel and his friends.

"At the end of the ten days they looked healthier and better nourished than any of the young men who ate the royal food. So, the guard took away their choice food and the wine they were to drink and gave them vegetables instead." Daniel 1:15-16 NIV

4. **Dominion:** God added special gifts and abilities to Daniel that would allow him to have dominion and be the solution to the problems of the king. Daniel may not have been king but we see that later in his journey every king trusted him with the decisions concerning the future of the land! He ruled without

WHAT IS A MAN?

even having the title of King! You don't need to be the PM or President to rule!

"To these four young men God gave knowledge and understanding of all kinds of literature and learning. And Daniel could understand visions and dreams of all kinds. At the end of the time set by the king to bring them into his service, the chief official presented them to Nebuchadnezzar. The king talked with them, and he found none equal to Daniel, Hananiah, Mishael and Azariah; so, they entered the king's service. In every matter of wisdom and understanding about which the king questioned them, he found them ten times better than all the magicians and enchanters in his whole kingdom." Daniel 1:17-20 NIV

This is a simple look at the way this mandate of God for all men has been used in action. There are some keys to it that will allow you to apply this in your life, in your career and maybe even in your job!

YOU DON'T ALWAYS NEED TO HAVE A HIGH PLACED TITLE TO RULE!

HOW TO HAVE DOMINION

1. Switch our focus

Many of us have the wrong focus, we have the wrong priorities. We have to understand that every environment we go into is an opportunity to rule for Christ! Your mandate is dominion, so it doesn't matter where you go, the mandate never changes. Let's stop making our priorities things like having a trophy wife, good life, a big house, and an expensive car! No! That's not it.

This needs to be your mindset and your focus, everywhere you go: **"How can I take control of this place for God?"**

WHAT IS A MAN?

2. Be ruthless

I know this may be a word that may not seem very Christian, but it is necessary for us to use when it comes to you fulfilling your mandate. If you're supposed to rule the earth, it means the enemy is not going to be your friend, but as long as you are happy to allow the earth to stay as it is and for life to dictate to you what you can achieve, then you are allowing the enemy to rob you of destiny and purpose. Your race is to rule this earth, so run that! Do not try to run anyone else's race, what is it that God has ordained for you to do and where? Once you know this you need to be focused and get to it, no excuse.

3. Understand your position

Your position is a joint heir with Christ which means you need to walk with a different posture to just any other man that isn't a believer. You have been given dominion by God in your creation but you have also been empowered to have dominion wherever you go! It is up to you to walk in it, to harness it and make it manifest on earth! As a son of God, you have the authority through the name of Jesus, to speak to anything and it should bow! You don't need to earn the right to rule the earth you have inherited it! That is your position!

4. Think bigger

"Believe Big. The size of your success is determined by the size of your belief. Think little goals and expect little achievements." David Schwartz

This is so key, you need to be able to understand that dominion is not a small thing, it is not for the small minded. Dominion requires you to think big, it requires you to believe that you can conquer whatever comes your way, it requires you to believe the word that is said over you. Some may say the statement;

WHAT IS A MAN?

believe *in your sauce* and this makes sense because God wouldn't create you to rule if you were not capable of doing it.

Let's not just think about being in an industry, let's start to think about dominating industries! If you're a sportsperson, don't settle for being just in it, think about being the best and dominating that sport! That is what you are called to do. Change your expectation from success to domination.

RECAP

A) Dominion is why you were created
B) Dominion is a result of being fruitful, multiplying and subduing the earth.
C) Dominion requires you to walk in the authority and power you have through Christ.
D) When you are walking in the mandate of God, He can and will give you dominion over what you face.
E) You are in that industry, job, school, or career to be the best!

WHAT IS A MAN?

Space for reflection

When reading this chapter and reviewing your life is there anything that you have noticed that stands out to you? Is there anything that has helped answer any questions you had about manhood? Use the space below to note anything down that you need to.

WHAT IS A MAN?

Myth #2: MEN DON'T CRY

Welcome to one of the most toxic myths and stereotypes we have created for men in this generation. There is too much emphasis on false masculinity and masculinity being emphasised by physical strength and inability to show emotions.

What I find interesting is that society has nothing to measure manliness by. If you don't cry when your grandma dies then you're a psycho, but if you cry when you're stressed or life is getting on top of you, then you're a wimp! This is the problem with societal standards, they actually don't make sense. Let's look at a scripture that shows us that men in fact do cry;

"Jesus wept." John 11:35 NIV

Jesus was the perfect man and He wept in pain, in sorrow, and in deep hurt! The love and care He had for Lazarus meant that He was touched in His heart when he had died originally. As men I believe we need to focus on being more like God, and there are characteristics that God has that we look at in this book, that make Him a great father that many of us would consider to be unmanly and Jesus shows one here when He wept.

Weeping is an expression of deep love not a sign of weakness! Real men show their emotions because they have true access to them, they are not suppressing them to maintain an image.

SECTION 4: PERSONAL DOMINION

"The process of reaching complete wholeness and dominion within and over self!"
Definition from Ira Jackson Jr

WHAT IS A MAN?

Many of you will not have heard of this before, but the Bible actually give us the formula for personal dominion. Adam is the perfect example of this as not only did he go through this process but he is actually the first man in the bible. Adam was God's perfect intention for a man and his journey up until the fall is exactly the way that God planned for life to be for a man. This means we can take a lot from this and look at it this as something we can and should live by, it's called in theology "The Law of First Mention".

Personal dominion can be further understood as the process of time and development that brings you to a place of wholeness and true direction in life. It provides you with the best platform and foundation to have a successful life and have successful relationships – being the best man you can be!

As a man you have a responsibility to make sure your life is in order, and this process is the **only way** to do that in the biblical sense. Many of us want to skip stages in life, allowing life and society to dictate to you what success is as a man.

Many relationships are fractured because the man doesn't have any direction, or purpose and they don't know their place which has a negative effect on their choices and their future. Whether you are a man or a woman, you need to go through the process of personal dominion.

It takes two people walking out and completing this process to be able to make a great partnership and marriage. It is not a limited process to those preparing for relationships but also those who may currently be in them or who have previously been in them and wondered what went wrong!

This process is something that allows you to focus on yourself but also to measure where someone is at in their journey of growth and maturity. This is why I have refrained from

WHAT IS A MAN?

mentioning anything about age, because it's nothing to do with age but is **more to do with stage**!

If we understand that relationships are a responsibility and fatherhood is a responsibility, then we will understand the necessity for personal dominion.

Everything you are about to read is going to shift your perspective on your priorities as a man. Before you are ready for any big commitments, or if you have already made them there is still hope. Now you have a criteria for personal growth, you can begin working on the areas where you are deficient or may have missed out due to the influence of the world.

PROCESS OF PERSONAL DOMINION

1. Place
2. Purpose
3. Parameters and Protocols
4. Patience in Preparation
5. Power

Through time we have become a people obsessed with relationships, with goals and with achieving societal targets and trends; which has led us to a place of imbalance and confusion. Something that informs our journey of personal dominion, is our inception on the earth, where did it all begin and how did we come about? That is what can give us a great platform to walk in personal dominion in our lives.

Let's look at Genesis 2:7 because this is something every man needs to understand about themselves before they walk the journey of personal dominion:

"Then the Lord God formed a man from the dust of the ground and breathed into his nostrils the breath of life, and the man became a living being." Genesis 2:7 (NIV)

WHAT IS A MAN?

You may be thinking what the relevance of this is but it is important for us to look at this and really understand it and how it informs your life. Many of us jump into relationships because we don't know our value or we are looking for a source of affirmation from somewhere to make us a man, to make us worthy. But God says right here that you are God breathed! You have been made a living being by God! Every breath that you breath is as a result of God giving you life, so this means that no one on this earth is responsible for giving you life, except the obvious person of your mom physically bringing you into this world.

Let's begin on this journey of personal dominion...

PLACES PLEASE

WHAT IS A MAN?

Before the start of any play, there is always the director or stage manager that says these two words **"Places Please!"** In order to let the actors, know that they need to get ready to go. It is important that the actors get in the right places to be able to perform their roles. As a man you are the actor in your life, you are the one acting the lead role in the process of what God has already predestined and orchestrated to be your life, the movie that you are the star of, but you have a responsibility, and that responsibility is to make sure that you are in the right place first and foremost.

The best place to begin when talking about personal dominion is place. Many of us as men struggle with this concept of place, we ask ourselves questions like this often:

1. What is my place?
2. Am I in the right place?
3. Where is my place?

I believe that this chasm, is a big problem for many of us as men and we end up using relationships as a filler to this place of indecision. So let me clear things up for you, place is the beginning of personal dominion.

1. WHAT IS PLACE?

The definition of place that we are going to use in this book is different to what you may be used to, because place is multi-dimensional; place means **your position in Christ** as well as meaning **your location and assignment**. So although both are location based, one is spiritual and the other is natural.

You need to know your place before anything in life, these questions have to be a surety before you bring anyone else into your life. When we look at this, the first thing we have to do is go to the Word, and Adam is always going to be the best person for

WHAT IS A MAN?

us to look at, in Genesis 2. God literally set out this formula and step by step process for us to learn from and live by.

The first thing we see here is that **God placed man**! In Genesis 2:15 we see here that God took Adam and he put him in the garden; the reason why he is there is not yet important, but the fact that he had a place in the first place. He was exactly where God wanted him to be; many of us complain about where we are in life, where we have come to, but have we ever stopped to think, is this where God wants me? Or better still, is this where God placed me?

"The Lord God took the man and put him in the Garden of Eden to work it and take care of it." Genesis 2:15 NIV

Your Place matters to God, so it should matter to you too! Just like Adam, God has picked you up and placed you somewhere! Do you think you were born in that area by accident? Do you think you were born into that family by accident? Do you think you work at that place by accident? Do you think this is all one big coincidence or is it all part of a bigger plan that God has that is laced with purpose? Follow me on this journey of personal dominion and you will see that this isn't a coincidence but a process that allows you to reach a place within yourself and in life where you are ready for the next chapter of your life.

2. AM I IN THE RIGHT PLACE?

This may be a foreign concept to some, but I believe that the spiritual place informs the natural place. Adam needed to have discernment or the place with Christ where he knew that the place he was being placed, was where he was supposed to be. God wouldn't have just placed him anyone there. Your position with Christ is so vital to understand, you, just like Adam are one with Christ as a believer, but that should inform you to walk in the ways of God and walk in what God has placed you in. This question is probably one of the most frequent questions that gets

WHAT IS A MAN?

asked when things get tough in any place, when things don't look like they were expected to, when things aren't perfect. We tend to ask ourselves the question: is this the right place? Is this really where God called me to be? Trials are not always an indicator of the wrong placement but they can be, and Jonah is an example of that.

The only real way you are going to know if you are in the right place is by having a close relationship with God, being able to hear and discern His voice and then act according to it. Many of us are struggling to discern because we don't know that God is intentional, we are restless, we are taking ourselves places that aren't in alignment with where God would want us and then wondering why everything seems to be crumbling around us.

There are a few things that you can notice that happen when you are **"out of place"**:

A) You are out of line with assignment

"But Jonah ran away from the Lord and headed for Tarshish. He went down to Joppa, where he found a ship bound for that port. After paying the fare, he went aboard and sailed for Tarshish to flee from the Lord." Jonah 1:3 NIV

B) Those around you begin to be negatively affected

"Then the Lord sent a great wind on the sea, and such a violent storm arose that the ship threatened to break up. All the sailors were afraid, and each cried out to his own god. And they threw the cargo into the sea to lighten the ship. But Jonah had gone below deck, where he lay down and fell into a deep sleep." Jonah 1:4-5 NIV

WHAT IS A MAN?

C) Your journey is delayed and troublesome

"Then the sailors said to each other, "Come, let us cast lots to find out who is responsible for this calamity." They cast lots and the lot fell on Jonah. So, they asked him, "Tell us, who is responsible for making all this trouble for us? What kind of work do you do? Where do you come from? What is your country? From what people are you?"" Jonah 1:7-8 NIV

D) You end up being thrown out of that place

"Then they took Jonah and threw him overboard, and the raging sea grew calm. At this the men greatly feared the Lord, and they offered a sacrifice to the Lord and made vows to him." Jonah 1:15-16 NIV

As we can see here from Jonah; when you are out of place, you won't just feel out of place but instead you will look out of place! Jonah was the reason the boat was going through trouble and those men's lives were in danger. A lot of us know our place but because of our own personal preference, pride, insecurity, or immaturity we neglect our place and choose another one, then we wonder why all of these things end up happening to us. You can't fulfil assignment if you're not in the place (location) you have been called to be in!

If you ever question whether you are in the right place, check to see if you disobeyed God and chose your own place and then also check to see if this A-D is happening to you. It is never too late to go to God and repent because as we see at the end of Jonah 1; God already has a failsafe in store for you to allow you to realign, reset and redirect.

WHAT IS A MAN?

3. WHERE IS MY PLACE?

This question is the question that should really be asked first before we get ourselves into anything, but this question is informed by knowing the answer to the first question, *"What is Place?"* If you know your position in Christ, it allows you to have the relationship with Him where you know His instruction is for your success and growth which allows you to seek His wisdom on your locational place and your assignment in that place.

MY ASSIGNMENT IS PLACED WHERE I AM PLACED!

Where has God placed you? Have you ever thought of that? Like your place is your territory, it is the place where God has called you to have dominion. So something you need to do before anything is to find out from God; where do you want me? Where am I called to? Your place could be an industry, it could be a country, it could be a sector, but you will never know unless you know to ask God that question, and the best time to find that out is before a relationship because you are only responsible for yourself and your future.

Too many of us are struggling in life because we don't know where our place is. We are struggling to progress, we are struggling in situations and it's not because we are not working hard enough or that we're not good enough, a lot of the time it is due to being in the wrong place. As Jonah showed, trouble follows you when you're in the wrong place, like everything just seems to go wrong and it is important that you understand if you don't know where you are supposed to be you have no right to bring someone on that journey! The sad thing as well is that someone reading this or that you know is married, has kids and they still don't know where their place is.

I'm here to encourage you, that God is calling you to greater, you don't have to make this mistake! You need to know that before you start thinking of anything, anyone or making any future

WHAT IS A MAN?

plans, I need to know where God has placed me because that sets the basis for everything else to flourish and build from. Us as men get distracted so easily by beautiful women when we are ***"out of place"*** and it leads to our thoughts and actions being out of place. We worry about something that isn't even in the right time, like you're not in the place to be in a relationship and you're not at the place either. There is nothing wrong with knowing you're not in the right place yet to engage in a relationship, it is actually better that way, because it means you are saving her heartache and your delay of purpose.

When you're not in the right place you being to think that everything is where it is supposed to be, you don't reflect, discern or analyse, you just assume that this is how it is supposed to be. You begin to invest in things that aren't meant for you and then you see that sin begins to follow you because you have left yourself open to it, by being out of place. Don't forfeit the area you are called to; don't forfeit the industry you are called to and don't forfeit the streams you are called to by walking into the wrong place.

WHEN THERE IS PLACEMENT THERE IS PURPOSE!

RECAP

- Personal dominion starts with a placement
- Submit to God placing you where he needs to place you

"If you aren't submitted to God how can you expect someone to submit to you"

- Have a relationship with God that allows you to discern and decipher where he is placing you
- Have a desire for God's assignment on your life and make that your focus

"What did God do first after he made Adam, He placed Him! So now that you are alive – find your place"

- Understand that you are placed for purpose

WHAT IS A MAN?

Space for reflection

When reading this chapter and reviewing your life is there anything that you have noticed that stands out to you? Is there anything that has helped answer any questions you had about manhood? Use the space below to note anything down that you need to.

WHAT IS A MAN?

THE PURPOSE EXPERIENCE

The next stage of the journey that we are on, is to find and understand purpose. We now know that where there is place there is purpose but what actually is purpose? What's so special about it? We know it's a buzz word that everybody uses, like people always ask like "What is my purpose?" we see things like Purpose coaches, we even see people who say things like **"I didn't know what my purpose was in life and then I…"** We have become so obsessed with finding purpose, but have we really stopped to think about what it actually is and what puts us in the best position to fulfil it.

According to Oxford Languages, purpose is **"the reason for which something is done or created or for which it exists."**

The biggest question many people want to know the answer to is **"What is my purpose?"** And there really is only one answer to that! I am going to explain it to you in an anecdotal form:

> You have a new mobile phone and you don't know how to work it fully, there's still some functions that you're trying to get the hang of and there's some apps that you don't know their purpose. So just like anyone in this generation, you decide to go onto social media or google and find out if someone can help you, and they give you some suggestions and then someone else gives you contrary suggestions and you end up being confused with what the purpose of these apps are. Then you go to the box, and in the box there is a little booklet which was written by the manufacturer and in that are the different functions of the phone, how to charge it and various other specific details from the manufacturer themself, giving you all the answers you need to use the phone the way it was intended to be used. Better still they also give you a link to their website where you can see a breakdown of each of the apps that come with the phone and all the features. You are now relaxed and equipped to use the phone to its fullest potential and purpose.

WHAT IS A MAN?

This story is exactly how we should see purpose. We can go to as many people as we like to ask them about our purpose but truly the only person that knows our purpose is our manufacturer. That manufacturer is God, the one who made you, designed you and purposed you before you were even born.

In order to delve more into purpose, we will continue in Genesis 2:15 and look toward the end of the verse for our understanding of purpose and its necessity in our lives to direct us and inform our actions.

"Then the Lord God took the man and put him in the garden of Eden to tend and keep it."

God placed Adam in the garden and then he gave him a purpose and that was to **tend** and to **keep** the place that he was put in.

Adam's purpose was twofold. It is interesting that there is an order to this process, even when we look at it scripturally; the place comes first but the placement has a purpose. There is a reason why you are placed where you are placed.

YOUR WHERE ALWAYS HAS A WHY!

If you direct yourself to a place where there is no clear purpose then abuse is often prevalent and therefore a life without purpose is a life misused. The key is that God placed Adam in the garden he didn't place himself!

Something many people don't know is that purpose is two things: as a believer it is *generic* but more importantly it is *multidimensional*.

1. **PURPOSE IS GENERIC**

The second you become a believer you share a purpose with every single other believer that there is, you were put on this

WHAT IS A MAN?

earth to be a living breathing reflection of God. This is something that is pretty generic and everyone who has been a believer for a while will know that we are called to evangelise and bring people to God through our lifestyle.

PURPOSE OF A MAN

We see with Adam as the first man, God's intention for man, that there is also generic purpose for every man; which is to tend and keep. Now we know this, it is essential to establish what that means specifically for us as men and how we can walk in that purpose as a basis.

A) Tend - abad (aw-bad):
- To Dress it
- To work
- To serve
- To labour

Some of you reading this when it said tend, might have been thinking; *"Is this a bar? What do you mean tend?"* But fortunately we have definitions and I am going to explain. There is some context to the word tend and bar-tend because it is **all about service**. As man you are called and purposed to labour and serve wherever God has placed you and we know that God doesn't just place you in workplaces but he also places you in families, churches, friendship groups, universities. You have to know your basic purpose there and what that looks like in each of those environments. Wherever you go, you have to work, and you have to serve! That is part of your purpose!

I guess now the statement is making sense where people say something has to *"serve its purpose"* because its purpose is to serve! Your purpose involves service!

The first thing God did to Adam after he gave him a place was give him a purpose and that was to work! Adam was given the

WHAT IS A MAN?

responsibility and the privilege of serving in the Garden of Eden! We then see for the remainder of that chapter that Adam is perfectly placed to receive more and more instruction from God, but his main focus is to walk in that purpose that God has given him. He wasn't thinking about anything else apart from pursuing and persisting in purpose.

In the environment that you are in; you are called to work, that might not just mean working in terms of getting a job, but it could come in the firm of serving in church, it could mean serving your family. Whatever it is you have to understand that as a man your purpose includes work and labouring, so it is something you are going to have to get used to doing and see it as a privilege that your purpose is to labour on behalf of God wherever you are!

A question you may need to ask yourself is **"Do I have the heart of service?"** Many people love to be served but don't love to serve and in order for you to walk in the purpose of God for your life you need to be able to serve the setting you are in. How do you serve the season you are in? Do you serve your purpose?

Something that we need to learn to do as men is while we are pursuing specific life purpose in detail, we need to walk in the purpose God has set generically for you as a man. When you do this, it puts you in a position to show God that you are stewarding well and ready to receive more detailed instructions on the intricacies of what specific part you play in God's major plan.

B) Keep – shamar (shaw-mar):
- To guard
- To have charge
- To protect
- To watch

WHAT IS A MAN?

Where God has placed you, you have a responsibility to have charge over it, to protect it and watch over it! This is the purpose of a man, wherever you go whatever environment and sector you are placed, you have a responsibility. We can look at this in the context of the industry you are in whether through work or career; as a man of God, you have a purpose to keep that industry.

If you're a football player, you are called and purposed to take charge of that industry because an industry under the influence of you is an industry under the influence of God. When you go into environments, your purpose is to protect the purity of the environment, protect the growth of the environment. You being placed there, should mean that the environment is protected and watched over, you have the best interest of the environment at heart.

Or shall we bring it closer to home? Many of us as men wonder why in our families, we are expected to protect our siblings, why as a father we are expected to have charge and guard our kids, like we love the idea of that responsibility, but we didn't know it was our purpose! This is why it's so vital that us as men understand our purpose, because where there is no purpose there is room for abuse. Better still where there is no idea of purpose the door is open for abuse. Many families right now are seeing and experiencing the crisis of a lack of idea of purpose.

I'll explain; when the man doesn't know it's his job and his purpose to protect and guard those God has blessed him with or the family he has been placed over; he sees purpose as pressure instead of a privilege and therefore sometimes he buckles. Even the enemy knows the man's purpose is to guard and protect and that's why he comes for men! A man not convinced about his purpose and not rooted in it will be bound and then his goods will be spoiled. The goods can be anything, his house, his life, his resources, his family, his finances.

WHAT IS A MAN?

Just a note; ***don't let the enemy come and bind you!***

""Or again, how can anyone enter a strong man's house and carry off his possessions unless he first ties up the strong man? Then he can plunder his house." Matthew 12:29 NIV

2. PURPOSE IS MULTIDIMENSIONAL

When you hear the word multidimensional what do you hear? What does it mean to you? How do you think it relates to purpose? We are going to look at Jesus as an example of how your specific God-given purpose can be multidimensional and what that means.

Multidimensional means *"something of or involving several dimensions."*

Your God-given purpose takes many forms and has many layers. An iPhone is also a classic example of multidimensional purpose; the original purpose of an iPhone, just like any other phone, is to make calls and take calls but it also serves many other purposes. You can write documents, read books, play games, video call people, run a business, buy stuff. This is a natural and simple example of how purpose can be multidimensional because these functions support the main purpose either to make it possible or to compliment it.

Back to Jesus really quick to look at this in human form, the Word of God says in 1 John 3:8:

"The one who does what is sinful is of the devil, because the devil has been sinning from the beginning. The reason the Son of God appeared was to destroy the devil's work." 1 John 3:8 NIV

So, this is Jesus' purpose, this is the reason he came to the earth, primarily! But then we get the question of, *"Ok, so what*

WHAT IS A MAN?

about all the stuff that he did then, like healing people?" And it is necessary for that question to be answered and that is how we know purpose is multidimensional because there were so many things that Jesus did as part of His purpose; many things that complimented that purpose. Let's even look at some of them;

- Healed the sick
- Cured the lame
- Opened blind eyes
- Cast out demons
- Died on the cross
- Led disciples
- Preached the gospel
- Fed the 5,000

All of this was part of His purpose and we may think that's a lot, but it was all necessary. If he didn't do that, we would have a land and generation of people who were unaffected because He wasn't walking in His purpose.

Do you understand how powerful your purpose is? On this journey of understanding and walking in personal dominion you're going to see how vital purpose is to the whole process.

The other aspect of purpose being multidimensional is the fact that it affects and informs so many different things in life. We find out from Jesus here that His purpose came with **power**, it came with **responsibility** and it affected **people**.

Going back to our main man at the start of the bible, Adam, God placed him and gave him a purpose and we see the multidimensional nature of that purpose continue to unfold. When God gives you a purpose, he is entrusting you with a responsibility to steward over that purpose, which is part of a greater purpose. He is giving you the power to be able to affect the world by you doing what you're called to do. Also, he is

WHAT IS A MAN?

giving you the permission to be able to use what he has given you to affect people's lives.

YOU WERE CREATED ON PURPOSE, BY PURPOSE, WITH PURPOSE AND TO SERVE A PURPOSE!

RECAP

- You were created by purpose, on purpose, for a purpose and with purpose!
- Purpose is a responsibility to steward
- Purpose comes with power to influence
- Purpose is permission to affect other lives
- Finding purpose can only be done through the manufacturer
- Every place has a purpose

WHAT IS A MAN?

Space for reflection

When reading this chapter and reviewing your life is there anything that you have noticed that stands out to you? Is there anything that has helped answer any questions you had about manhood? Use the space below to note anything down that you need to.

WHAT IS A MAN?

ORDER COMING RIGHT UP!

You may be wondering why the title is called *"order coming right up"* and I just want to let you know the original title was nothing like this, actually it was completely the opposite. The first title was called *"Don't touch that!"* But when I was finalising the chapter God began to speak and the Holy Spirit inspired this new title. What we are going to be studying through this is the idea that your steps are ordered by God, and you have to receive orders, in order to walk in purpose correctly.

Imagine you're a waiter; when you are at a restaurant serving your manager may say to you, *"you have freedom in this role, you can sit with the customers, you can have fun and enjoy conversation, just make sure you don't ever have any drinks with customers while you're on job!"* You have been given freedom, but you have a certain restriction because the manager knows what's best for you and has seen cases before where waiters have got too comfortable with their customers and then either been robbed, got drunk or missed out on serving other tables and then got fired. It is your job as the employee to make sure that you are in the right position to receive this information and understand that the boss isn't trying to be mean or oppressive but instead, he sees the bigger picture... this order that you have been given is to help you to fulfil purpose.

God even says in the Word that the steps of a righteous man are ordered; so if God places you, if you know your place with Christ and He has given you purpose, you would be considered righteous, so order is needed and also inevitable to your growth and development.

"The steps of a good man are ordered by the Lord: and he delighteth in his way." Psalms 37:23 KJV

So far when it comes to personal dominion, we know that God gives you a place and then he gives you a purpose for that place!

WHAT IS A MAN?

Our lives should be a constant pursuit of walking out of purpose, in whatever places we are placed because it won't just be one place for life. We are put into different types of places as we live this life on earth, and it is about having such a relationship with God that allows us to discern the purpose for each place.

Wouldn't it be good to know what happens when you are in that place? Well, that is something that I also wondered and wanted to study the Word to find the answer for. Like, when I begin walking in purpose is that it? Do I just get to do what I want, how I want as long as I end up fulfilling purpose? Let's be real this is something we need to make sure we understand and know because if we don't as men our humanity will cause us to be lawless and act out of the will of God. Then God gave me the revelation from the story of Adam and how it links to personal dominion.

We continue onto Genesis 2:16 where we see God gives some instructions as to what needs to be understood next in the pursuit of personal dominion; and that is **order** which many have also called the **parameters!**

"And the Lord God commanded the man, "You are free to eat from any tree in the garden; but you must not eat from the tree of the knowledge of good and evil, for when you eat from it you will certainly die."" Genesis 2:16-17 NIV

We can see here that God has given Adam a place, he's given him a purpose but then he's made sure to give him some instructions. I call this **Freedom within structure** because God is providing you with the freedom and empowerment to complete purpose, but he gives orders to give structure and allow you to continue to fulfil that purpose. God literally says, **"You can do and have everything except this!"** Now we have to ask ourselves the question why would he want us to not touch something, do something or be involved in something specific. The answer is simple; God knows what's best for you and wants

WHAT IS A MAN?

what's best for you so there may be some things that he needs to keep you from in order to keep you for purpose!

GOD GAVE ADAM PARAMETERS!

God wouldn't be a great father if he didn't implement some sort of structure, and we know this because even our parents do this. ***"You can go to the party and enjoy yourself, just make sure you don't get yourself into any trouble or get drunk!"*** Is this not the same? You have been given the freedom, but you have been given freedom within structure because your parents knew what could potentially happen if you had too much to drink.

If we don't have structure, we will end up doing what we want, not because we are bad but because we are naturally inquisitive and we like to experience and experiment. If we see something that is attractive our natural sense is to want it without weighing up the benefits and costs of it. This is why God did what he did, if we aren't told that we have access to everything we will assume we are missing out, which will lead us to desire what we think we are missing more.

God in His supreme wisdom made sure he informed Adam ***"you can eat from any tree"*** so if we look at it in the context of now; God could be telling you ***"you have access to all the money in the world except…"*** In order for us to walk out our purpose in these parameters without disobeying God. Trust can be built on both sides when we have boundaries; God needs to know that he can trust us with the instructions that he gives us, but we also need to be able to know that God's instructions are with our best intentions at heart. We see that they are at the end of verse 17 because God tells Adam why he doesn't want him touching the tree ***"when you eat it you will certainly die!"***

GOD DOESN'T WANT YOU TO DIE, SO HE GIVES YOU PARAMETERS TO PREVENT THAT FROM HAPPENING.

WHAT IS A MAN?

ORDER

What we see in Genesis 2:16-17 is an order from God, an instruction, a command being given to Adam that we can take and learn from for our own journey of personal dominion, to help us to stay focused on growing in purpose.

The word command in Hebrew is translated as **tsavah** pronounced **(tsaw-vaw)** and some of the definitions for it are:

- To charge
- To appoint
- To order
- To give orders
- To give charge

Something that I noticed about God giving Adam this order is that he also established an order in this process.

WHEN GOD GIVES AN ORDER, HE IS ALSO ESTABLISHING AN ORDER!

God is the person who gives the orders for you in your life, he is the director of the movie and he is giving you the instructions to be able to be able to carry out your life and purpose in the best way you can, and he is the best person to do it because he knows everything! As men this is essential that we understand and grow in this on our journey of personal dominion because one day you are going to be leading a family and if you don't know the order of God how are you going to establish it within your family. If you aren't led by God how are you going to lead a family?

What orders have you been given by God? What has God commanded you to do and not to do? Begin to think about these things because you could be struggling now because you haven't respected the order of God in your life. You could be struggling

WHAT IS A MAN?

as a parent because you don't know the order of God, you haven't allowed God to establish order in your life, you haven't allowed God to lead you and that's why you are struggling to lead your family. Maybe, just maybe your struggles in purpose and in life are because you aren't walking in order!

GOD DOESN'T WANT TO RESTRICT YOU; HE WANTS TO RELEASE YOU!

You need to have a relationship with God, you need to trust God, you need to hear God, in order to discern and decipher the instructions He is giving you. God knows the things that are not going to be of benefit to you in your walk and in your life of purpose. This idea of following orders may be a foreign concept to some men, that we have to *"sit down and be humble"* as Kendrick Lamar says and receive instructions that allow us to walk out purpose more effectively but it is necessary so that you don't die, and your purpose doesn't die.

"The fear of the Lord is the beginning of knowledge, but fools despise wisdom and instruction." Proverbs 1:7 NIV

As this scripture says; don't be a fool and ignore what is going to keep you alive or help you to progress in purpose.

IDENTITY

When I began to look at this scripture more and more and began to really pray over it; understanding what is behind it as well as what we can see on the paper, God began to really unravel something that was so profound. He revealed the idea that identity is linked to the orders that God gives you. Identity is a key in the process of personal dominion.

When God said to Adam, that he would really die, we need to understand that God isn't talking about physical death, but He is talking about the death of purpose, the death to identity, the

WHAT IS A MAN?

death of trust, the death of Adam's spirit because he has lost **HIMSELF**! Many of us lose our identity, because we don't understand the orders of God, we chase things when God tells us we don't need to. We assume that our identity is in money, in positions, or in accolades, but your identity is only in Him! When we go chasing these things, this is what God is talking about!

Sometimes God may place you in a workplace with a purpose to be an impact for Him and win souls and He may give you an instruction to not worry about money at this job; because you aren't there to become a millionaire but to learn the things that you need to learn to grow, and to prepare for when He releases you into your next. If you then go to chase money and promotions and begin praying for hours into how you can get promoted you are ignoring the instructions of God and are shaping your life and your identity on how much money you are earning and this is where you lose yourself, because you have disobeyed God and forsaken your identity.

GOD'S INSTRUCTIONS ARE TO AFFIRM AND CONFIRM YOUR IDENTITY.

As a man it is extremely important that you don't lose your identity, because generations are supposed to be led by you, you are the head of a house, you are responsible for shaping so many futures, that it is vital that you know who you are and that you know God's intentions behind His instructions. There is a reason why He keeps you from certain things; because your identity doesn't come from a home, it doesn't come from money, it doesn't come from sex! Your identity is in Him and His intention when creating you! All He has placed in you is all you need; He doesn't need you looking for other things to find yourself. If He instructs you not to do something it is because He has given you everything you need to have a successful life and to fulfil purpose!

WHAT IS A MAN?

RECAP

- When God places you not only will He give you a purpose, but he will also give instructions with that!
- When God gives an order, He establishes an order!
- Trust is an essential key to understanding order; know God's intentions behind His instructions!
- God's instructions are to affirm and confirm your identity.
- Personal dominion can be hindered by disobedience to the orders and instructions of God
- The "You shall surely die" Death is not physical but a loss of self, identity, and purpose.

WHAT IS A MAN?

Space for reflection

When reading this chapter and reviewing your life is there anything that you have noticed that stands out to you? Is there anything that has helped answer any questions you had about manhood? Use the space below to note anything down that you need to.

WHAT IS A MAN?

PATIENCE IS A VIRTUE

I hope that this last chapter hasn't got you in a mood, before you read this one because as we are still on the journey of personal dominion, we still haven't mentioned anything about **"When do I meet my girl"** That is because you need to grow, you need to prepare, you need to gain momentum, you need to build wins with God before you get to the place of a new level of responsibility which we know is a relationship and this comes after personal dominion but as a by-product of successful personal dominion.

Cato the Elder stated in a Latin textbook that **"Of human virtues, patience is the greatest!"** Commonly known as **"Patience is a virtue"** in this generation. Have we ever really sat to think of this, and what it means? How important it might be for us to understand and live out?

Isn't it great that God created the bible and the process of dominion which would answer our questions at exactly the right time? He gives you a place, He informs you of purpose and then gives you some orders and parameters that allow you to stay on course to purpose and enjoy it without losing your identity.

So how does patience relate to the process of personal dominion, like what does it mean in the context of a man and his journey of personal dominion. God says something really interesting in Genesis 2:18 which we haven't seen before. God says it is not Good... but until it becomes good, there is a process of patience in preparation.

"The Lord God said, "It is not good for the man to be alone. I will make a helper suitable for him."" Genesis 2:18 NIV

God noticed that there was a problem in the journey of this man, we weren't meant to do life alone. So in order to rectify that, in order to make sure that Adam had a purpose partner He said He

WHAT IS A MAN?

would make one that suited him right down to the T. All this time that God is working on making the not good, good, Adam has to have patience and prepare to receive her. Adam has to make sure that he doesn't lose focus on his purpose, because there is a protocol in the process of personal dominion.

This is going to be the case in your life, that while you're on this journey of personal dominion, pursuing purpose, that God is going to say to himself that it is time for you to have help. As we see from Adam there is a certain level of personal dominion that needs to be reached where you are in that position to receive the blessing of the help that God has created for you.

Something that we have to see that shows us how important patience in preparation is, is where we know God can create things in an instant, but he took His time to create Eve. Eve wasn't created in an instant, like He saw the problem, but He allowed the man to continue to build and be patient and pursue purpose some more before she came so she could be prepared, and he could be prepared.

Many of us are rushing to find a person; without following the protocols, without finding purpose, without going through the process, without knowing our place. We need to know that God isn't silly, He knows that at some point a man would need a wife, He knew that purpose needs a partner, but He also knows that you need to be patient while she is being prepared. Don't try to force relationships, don't try to force preparation, don't disturb a woman who is in her stage of being prepared while you're being prepared.

WHAT IS A MAN?

Look at it like this:

> Let's imagine that this part of personal dominion is like having dinner. The woman is cooked food and you as the man are the person eating the food. The food is raw and needs to be cooked. Before it can be consumed, this takes 45 minutes so taking it out any time before that could be hazardous if you eat it it's at your own risk. This time that the food is being prepared for you to eat; you can set the table, get the plates ready, make sure that the complimentary pieces of the dish are ready, but the main thing is that you need to be patient while it is preparing. When the oven dings and the 45 minutes is up you take the food out and you are able to enjoy the meal because you were in the right position to receive it as the blessing it was, and it was well prepared to be nutritious and cooked for you to consume. If you were to take it out early, the obvious would happen, you are likely to get food poisoning and the food is likely to go in the bin. This is why it is so vital that you are patient in preparation because you don't want to mess up a woman or your own life because you have decided to be impatient.

A RELATIONSHIP IS NOT BAD IT JUST MIGHT NOT BE NECESSARY RIGHT NOW!

God knows you may need someone at some point, but He also knows that you need to be in a space to rightly receive the woman that God has for you!

This generation is probably the hardest generation to be patient in preparation because there are so many external influences that are going to be feeding you information that contradicts what God is saying. The acceptable age for relationships changes every three months based upon society but that is because they don't consider the phase in which you are being prepared in the

WHAT IS A MAN?

different aspects of your life to be ready to be what God has called you to be as a man to that woman that He is about to bless you with.

THE ART OF PATIENCE

Now, during this chapter so far, I have mentioned patience a lot, I have given you examples of why you should be patient, but I think the only way you are going to walk this out in your life and understand it in its fullness is if I explain to you the art of patience. How am I patient knowing that something big is coming? Because many of us struggle with this! Even Abraham and Sarah struggled so don't worry you're not alone in this journey of patience and maybe getting it wrong now and again.

When we look at the formula of patience from a Biblical lens, we see something like this:

> **PROBLEM + PROMISE + PATIENCE IN PREPARATION = PROMISE COMING TO PASS!**

A PROMISE IS GIVEN TO FIX A PROBLEM, BUT PATIENCE IN PREPARATION IS REQUIRED TO SEE THE PROMISE!

We see with Adam's situation that God noticed his lack of a partner was a problem and therefore He made a promise of making a helper and then it required Adam to be patient whilst the promise was being realised.

You will see this in the story of Abraham and Sarah and the promise God gave them, is that they would have a son! Let's look at their experience and learn how we can be patient in preparation.

The problem we see for Abraham and Sarah is that they are getting old and they have no children, in the biblical times, children were heirs to the throne, you were seen as blessed to

WHAT IS A MAN?

have them, which has seemed to lose its meaning in this generation but nonetheless, they didn't have kids so when God is telling Abram that he's going to receive blessings he isn't sure what the point is because he has no one to pass it on to. So here we have our **problem**!

"But Abram said, "Sovereign Lord, what can you give me since I remain childless and the one who will inherit my estate is Eliezer of Damascus?" And Abram said, "You have given me no children; so, a servant in my household will be my heir."" **Genesis 15:2-3 NIV**

So with every problem God brings a promise, this promise here is specific but has no time on it. God just says one day you will have a son, and this is something that we need to understand; sometimes God isn't going to tell you exactly when you will have something because the time that you are waiting you need to stay plugged into Him because He is the one who gave the promise. You need to consistently be plugged into Him and His plan along the process trusting the God of the promise to bring it to pass.

"Then the word of the Lord came to him: "This man will not be your heir, but a son who is your own flesh and blood will be your heir." He took him outside and said, "Look up at the sky and count the stars—if indeed you can count them." Then he said to him, "So shall your offspring be."" **Genesis 15:4-5 NIV**

The next part of the formula is where Abraham and Sarah both struggled and it is also where most of us as men struggle. Society has told us that if we are 21 and we don't have a girlfriend there must be something wrong, it has said if you're not having sex regularly then you're not a man, it has set some unrealistic and ever-changing criteria for what makes you ready for longer commitments or when you would be considered a man. Abraham suffered slightly in this area because he didn't feel

WHAT IS A MAN?

fulfilled without a child, he didn't feel like he had achieved if he had no one to pass things down to.

It is so hard in this generation to be patient as God is preparing you and your next chapter, we live in such a microwave society that you can go on a date without ever physically asking someone, you can swipe on an app and select what type of girl you like instead of actually going out and interacting with others and then being patient and doing your thing until the time is right. There seems to be no such thing as patience anymore, which will make us feel like Abraham and Sarah's situation is far too extreme, but there is something we can look at to see what we can do in our time of patience; what is the art of patience in preparation.

"So, after Abram had been living in Canaan ten years, Sarai his wife took her Egyptian slave Hagar and gave her to her husband to be his wife. He slept with Hagar, and she conceived. When she knew she was pregnant, she began to despise her mistress." Genesis 16:3-4 NIV

THE PROMISE IS NOT JUST TO FIX PROBLEMS BUT IT IS ALSO TO PREVENT FUTURE PROBLEMS!

What we see here in the story of Abraham is that the promise God gave him was to fix his issue of not having an heir, but his response along with the help and pressure of his wife to fulfil the promise for themselves, is what caused a future problem. This problem was not just what we see here between Hagar and Sarah but would eventually spring into issues for Ishmael, which the angel prophecies:

"The angel of the Lord also said to her: "You are now pregnant, and you will give birth to a son. You shall name him Ishmael, for the Lord has heard of your misery. He will be a wild donkey of a man; his hand will be against everyone and everyone's

WHAT IS A MAN?

hand against him, and he will live in hostility toward all his brothers."" **Genesis 16:11-12 NIV**

Some of you may be thinking **"Well what happens for me now, I am in the same place as Abraham, I think I've walked into something that isn't my promise because I was impatient, how do I deal with it?"** The Bible already has the answers for you because Abraham was literally in this situation and instead of God killing off Ishmael or withholding the promise of Isaac, he blessed them both and the promise still came to pass. This isn't a licence to disobey God, but it is an insight into the goodness and mercy of God. However, the consequences of actions are natural and they will come, in a lot of senses if you disobey God's promise and don't wait then often you will be in situations that may stop you from getting your promise like when it comes to a wife or something like that because God doesn't want to divorce you but that then may be a bad marriage because you rushed into it too soon which you may choose to end in a divorce! Later down the line God will still deliver the promise but there is something or there are somethings that need to be sorted before you receive a promise.

HOW TO BE PATIENT IN PREPARATION

1. Trust the God of the Process

Many of us love that phrase *"trust the process"* but what happens when you realise the process doesn't want you to fail or succeed. The process has no vested interest in you. This is what happens in our lives, we trust the process and then at some point the journey gets too hard and then we give up and try to create a counterfeit of what God promised us. God wants the best for us, and we have to know that and trust that, He has the best and perfect plans for us so if He has given the promise, we need to trust Him in and through the process of patience in preparation to receive it.

WHAT IS A MAN?

2. Think Focused not Forward

Many of us have become so obsessed with seeing the promise come to pass, with the when, the how, and all the particulars of the promise that we forget to be focused on the now. This time in preparation is the perfect time to be walking in purpose, to be pursuing purpose and building a record of wins with God. Develop the character and the fortitude needed to manage this next stage. How can I be preparing to receive this promise? What state will I be in character wise when the promise comes to pass? Will I be able to manage the promise? Will I be mature enough to be able to recognise the promise whatever way it comes? Have I created the right environment and space to manage and steward this promise?

3. Relinquish control and Refrain from interference

We love control as men, so when we are told to trust or to wait, we believe that means we need to help make that happen. We are so used to being hands on, but God's promise being fulfilled in your life doesn't need you accelerating it, it doesn't need you trying to make the connections to make it happen, it needs you to be patient. Stop getting restless, stop trying to figure out where the connection is going to come from, stop trying to manufacture a promise that you didn't even promise. Abraham interfered and ended up creating problems for himself and in his family.

4. Delay doesn't mean Denial

In this generation, we know that we live in a microwave society so it seems cross cultural that you would have to wait for anything, but you have to understand that the promise is worth having, so it may take time. The time it takes isn't an indicator that it isn't going to happen but instead a process that you have to go through, daily you are getting stronger, getting closer and being given the opportunity to get more prepared for when it

WHAT IS A MAN?

actually comes to pass. Delay can be a blessing if you look at in the right perspective.

RECAP

- God recognises the problem and is preparing your promise for you but you just need to be patient
- Trust God not the process and submit to whatever God needs to do in you while you are waiting
- You need to know the art of patience in order to not create a counterfeit promise
- The promise doesn't just fix a problem, but it prevents future problems!
- Relationships are not bad they may just not be for now!

WHAT IS A MAN?

Space for reflection

When reading this chapter and reviewing your life is there anything that you have noticed that stands out to you? Is there anything that has helped answer any questions you had about manhood? Use the space below to note anything down that you need to.

WHAT IS A MAN?

I'VE GOT THE POWER

Cue the music and the celebrations because we are at the last stage of personal dominion. You should be proud of yourself because you are so much closer to becoming the man of God that He has called you to be. As you can tell from the title of this chapter, this is about power and guess who is getting the power... it's you! So, make sure you keep reading this so that you can start to walk in personal dominion or complete your process of personal dominion.

This chapter is going to be all about power and responsibility! Anyone that has watched Spider-Man has seen that moment in the movie where Uncle Ben says to Peter **"With Great power comes Great responsibility!"** Many know this as the Peter Parker principle but in a roundabout way this is a biblical principle from the scripture in Luke 12:48 where it says:

"But the one who does not know and does things deserving punishment will be beaten with few blows. From everyone who has been given much, much will be demanded; and from the one who has been entrusted with much, much more will be asked." Luke 12:48 NIV

Before we look at this in more detail, let's go to the Word and see in our study of Adam and God's intention for personal dominion what this looked like for him.

"Now the Lord God had formed out of the ground all the wild animals and all the birds in the sky. He brought them to the man to see what he would name them; and whatever the man called each living creature, that was its name. So, the man gave names to all the livestock, the birds in the sky and all the wild animals. But for Adam no suitable helper was found." Genesis 2:19-20 NIV

WHAT IS A MAN?

As we see here, God created some new creatures and then brought them to Adam to name; whatever he called them is what they were to be! Now I don't know about you but that seems pretty cool to me... like the same voice activated power that God used to call the day-day and night-night; He gave to Adam and said whatever you feel like naming these things is what they will be! Not only had Adam been given the power to do it but he had been given the responsibility to do it! Adam had complete power, authority, and autonomy; he literally was God on earth! Wow... I can see your antenna's going up already, **"God on Earth? You know how powerful I would be? OMG!!!!"** Well before you get too excited let's understand the purpose of that and how it relates to a man and our process of personal dominion.

UNDERSTANDING THE POWER CHAIN

Something that we see from this and we need to understand is that us (Adam) don't get given power for the sake of it. We are called to be a reflection of God, which means as men at some point we are going to have to walk in that before we claim the position. God is the head of our lives and as men we are called to be the head of the house, so it means that before we have a house we need to learn, understand, and walk in that power! God giving Adam the power to name the animals was a specific move by God to establish a power chain in man that would allow Him to walk out every purpose he was called to!

Whatever God is preparing you for it is important that you understand that the power is used for a few purposes, so whether you are going into business, a new industry or into a marriage you need to understand that the power God gives is an empowerment:

- Power to do
- Power to establish
- Power to build
- Power to declare

WHAT IS A MAN?

- Power to name

God is giving you the same thing as well; God wants to give you His power so that you can walk as He has called you to walk, and the important thing is that you don't need to be married to have that power, God actually gives it to you before you even get to that stage. This is the key to personal dominion; you don't need anyone else to have personal dominion. No one else can walk your personal purpose for you.

GOD WILL ALWAYS PREPARE YOU FOR WHAT HE WANTS YOU TO BE RESPONSIBLE OVER BEFORE GIVING IT TO YOU!

This is something that many will struggle with because we just want what we want and we want it now, but God isn't stupid, He knows that you need to build momentum. Personal dominion is all about you developing what you need to develop on a personal level before you enter a marriage and build your family. You need to be able to walk in the power and authority of God before you bring a woman into your life. You need to know and walk in responsibility before you are responsible for a family!

We found in the last chapter that God recognised there was a problem with Adam being alone but didn't create Eve straight away. We then see this perpetuated here because God created animals in the next verses that we begin to read but He still doesn't create Eve. This must mean something, there must be a reason to this.

THE PURPOSE WITHIN THE POWER

Some may say that God created the animals because He wanted to see if they were comparable help to Adam. This is definitely a school of thought, but if we are to believe that God doesn't make mistakes as we know He doesn't, then why would He create something by accident? Some other people have the perspective that God created the animals because He is enough and Adam

WHAT IS A MAN?

didn't really need any human connection at that time because everything he had, he had in God, God was his ultimate companion. Again, this perspective has some validity, but God wouldn't say that it isn't Good for man to be alone if He didn't think there was a slight void there that even He couldn't fill! We were called to live on this Earth with other people. We were called to walk out life with people.

PURPOSE NEEDS PARTNERS!

We have to take context from both of these paradigms but look at them from a different perspective, which is something that God showed me when I was studying these scriptures to teach it to my mentees and something that I have already walked out in my life as well. Everything that God did before bringing Eve to Adam was to prepare him to meet her. There are so many things that he needed to know and understand and even be walking in before he met Eve because he needed to be the type of man that was ready to be the man that she was created to help!

If you want context then I'm going to fast forward a verse to show you how these things tie together and why they are needed to before you get yourself into a relationship.

***"Then the Lord God made a woman from the rib he had taken out of the man, and he brought her to the man. The man said, "This is now bone of my bones and flesh of my flesh; she shall be called 'woman,' for she was taken out of man.""* Genesis 2:22-23 NIV**

What we see here from Adam is him reaching personal dominion; when you read what he says about Eve when he meets her, that doesn't sound like a suggestion, that doesn't sound like he isn't sure, that sounds like he is calling things to be! He declares that Eve is his wife, but what informs this and what allows him to do this; it is the power that God had given him to name the animals.

WHAT IS A MAN?

The animals are just a taste of power, naming them as God named everything else in the Earth is the power of God in action through Adam! God gives Adam a preview of responsibility; being in charge of that many animals and having the responsibility to give them an identity and a name is something that he was going to need when he has kids.

In our life it may not be animals, but God may have taken you a new level of power and responsibility recently, has He given you a vision for a business, has He empowered you to begin mentoring, have you begun to walk in a deeper degree of leadership? These are some of the things that God does in this stage of personal dominion because as we know already, God is a God of momentum He wants to have you walking in what you will need before you receive it. We have to understand that love is a responsibility, and God even wants us to be prepared for that!

RESPONSIBILITY

Relationships are a responsibility, marriage is a responsibility, business is a responsibility, kids are a responsibility. How do you manage the responsibilities God has given? We know that God doesn't give you more than you could handle, so then God won't give you more responsibility than you are ready for. So could the reason be as to why you haven't found "your wife" because you aren't responsible enough. This period at the end of personal dominion is a combination of power and responsibility. Yes, God wants to empower you to do, to be, build and all of these things but He also wants to make sure you are responsible.

When you are in this stage; you still have a responsibility to be patient in preparation. But this patience is an active patience, walk in purpose, stay focused and don't wander but also steward the purpose you have been given (be faithful to serve the season that you are in) you are on the cusp, but you have a responsibility to your purpose more than you have a

WHAT IS A MAN?

responsibility to your partner because your purpose is your priority at this time not your partner.

Something you can be doing actively in this stage is be planted in the place that God has called you to be, don't go roaming around seeing if you can find what God has promised you, as we notice Adam didn't go anywhere. Spend this time building trust with God, building credit with God, and growing in your purpose which is all essential to becoming the man that you are called to be.

MANY OF US FOCUS ON GETTING THE GIRL OF OUR DREAMS WHEN WE SHOULD FOCUS ON BECOMING THE MAN, WE'RE SUPPOSED TO BE!

FINISHING TOUCHES

The final stage before receiving your wife, is preparing to be a husband, everything you have been doing up until this point has been preparing you to be a successful husband and someone worthy of help. In this stage of receiving power; you have to learn the art of declaration, because everything that Adam did when naming them animals was declare over them what they would be, and we parallel this with when you become a father, or a husband and you have the responsibility of declaring things over your wife and child. If you have never built this before marriage in the personal dominion stage, you won't be prepared to do it in marriage.

"The tongue has the power of life and death, and those who love it will eat its fruit." Proverbs 18:21 NIV

You need to learn the power that is running through your veins and in your mouth, God has handed you the power He possesses to be able to speak life into things, to be able to call things into being based upon His design and instructions. You need to know and walk in the fact that when you speak God speaks but you

WHAT IS A MAN?

must be walking in the fullness of your DNA, the blessing, the mandate and personal dominion to be doing this.

You need to understand the declarations that come from your mouth come with weight, and you have to be careful, especially when speaking over the things God has given you. Understand the responsibility that comes with the power that you carry; it is a responsibility to speak life, but God will give you an opportunity to do that in a controlled environment before He does that with you in a family. If you haven't cultivated the power of God in your life in the personal dominion stage, then how do you expect to have authority in a house or over a family? You can't, it is not possible.

When David went against Goliath, the only reason he was able to speak with the authority and power that he did was because he had been cultivating that in private with God when defeating the lions and the bear protecting his sheep. God prepared him in protecting and conquering in obscurity with animals, before he did that with people. This has been the same with Adam; God gets him to name and tend to a land with animals in it before he has to do the same thing for a wife and family. Is it starting to make sense now?

POWER IS CULTIVATED IN PREPARATION!

WHAT IS A MAN?

RECAP

- Everything you have done before finding Eve has prepared you to be a successful husband to Eve
- With Great power comes Great responsibility
- Even in the stage of receiving the power and responsibility from God that is still preparation
- Trust is built in this stage because God can affirm and confirm that you are ready for your next by how you steward your now
- Power is the force and authority of God at work within you to do, build, declare, establish and name

WHAT IS A MAN?

Space for reflection

When reading this chapter and reviewing your life is there anything that you have noticed that stands out to you? Is there anything that has helped answer any questions you had about manhood? Use the space below to note anything down that you need to.

WHAT IS A MAN?

Myth #3: ALL MEN CHEAT

Although this isn't entirely true, not all men cheat, us as men have lived with an air of arrogance. Cheating starts with a paradigm before it becomes an action; if you don't see a marriage as a covenant, if you don't see it as something you're called to steward, if you didn't have personal dominion before your marriage, if you didn't work on your character before marriage then you're going to find cheating acceptable and more than likely do it.

The paradigm pandemic goes deeper than the action of cheating; it begins with the idea that men are gods, now in the right context this is true because we are reflections of God but when we use this to be dishonourable and manipulative then it is wrong and ungodly. Men for centuries have believed they are above the law, and this mentally is the beginning of cheating.

"A woman that cheats is a hoe, a man that cheats is just a man!"

WHATEVER YOU DON'T CONFRONT YOU CONSENT!

This is what we need to do as men; we need to globally tackle confront the paradigm of pride, double standards, manipulation, lust, greed and then we beat the pandemic of cheating!

"Marriage should be honoured by all, and the marriage bed kept pure, for God will judge the adulterer and all the sexually immoral." Hebrews 13:4 NIV

WHAT IS A MAN?

SECTION 5: CHARACTER

"the mental and moral qualities distinctive to an individual."
Definition from Oxford Languages

WHAT IS A MAN?

A FLAWED FOUNDATION

We are about to touch on a subject that is severely missed when we look at men in general. We have said earlier in the book that men struggle with identity but something that is a cancer in this gender is the dismissal and refusal to have standards when it comes to **character**. This isn't just outside of the church; this is inside the church as well. Many of the men of God that we know are phenomenally skilled, they are gifted, articulate but they lack in an area that matters more than any gifting and that is character. Character keeps you in places that your gift cannot keep you! Many people reach a level based on their gift but when they have to live and stay at that level character is then seen, proven, or even exposed.

Let's even bring this closer to home and bear in mind this isn't to bash anybody or make anyone feel bad, but it is to really put a magnifying glass up to men as a whole whether in the church or not and begin to examine character. We see so often in the news, that people we looked up to, whether that be pastors, footballers, presidents, are being exposed for their lack of character and how that is displayed in their actions. For many of us that disheartens us because we assume that social status means they have character when it really doesn't. As we have seen gifting is tested and scrutinised on the way up but character very rarely is.

What I want to do is present to you some character keys, some tips, some examples, some insight into character and how that looks as a man of God. This is a standard for you to measure yourself and others by that is based upon the Word and not anyone's opinion. If you want to be a man of God and a man of character, then it is essential that you take these keys on board and make sure to apply them and constantly measure yourself, or better still, assess yourself honestly by the Word. The Word is the only unchanging standard you will ever come across and Jesus is the best and perfect standard of what a man is

WHAT IS A MAN?

supposed to look like in terms of character and conduct. We're going to take some inspiration and insight from Him and His life to see how He; fully God and fully man managed to live a life of character.

WHAT BETTER PLACE TO LOOK THAN JESUS!

According to Webster's revised unabridged dictionary, character is:

"The peculiar quality, or the sum of qualities, by which a person or a thing is distinguished from others; the stamp impressed by nature, education, or habit; that which a person or thing really is nature; disposition."

We are going to start at the beginning when it comes to character, we have a definition but we also need to understand the foundation of it, what it looks like biblically and then how we can start to live a life of character.

The foundation of character is being one with God and submitted to His Word. The Word says in Joshua 1:8 something that we don't equate to character but when you actually read it, it is so important to help and shape character.

"Keep this Book of the Law always on your lips; meditate on it day and night, so that you may be careful to do everything written in it. Then you will be prosperous and successful." Joshua 1:8 NIV

Character needs to be founded on the Word and needs to be submitted to God and the place we will see a perfect example of this is in Matthew 4:1-11. Jesus is being tempted by the enemy and given the opportunity to sin, the opportunity to meet a need He had whilst losing His soul but He stood firm and we are going to study this as an introduction to character, before we start looking at some character traits that a man of God needs.

WHAT IS A MAN?

CHARACTER WILL BE TESTED

"Then Jesus was led by the Spirit into the wilderness to be tempted by the devil." Matthew 4:1 NIV

I believe that this passage of scripture is a phenomenal example and template of how us as believers need to navigate the waves and wizardry of this world and maintain character that reflects God. Jesus did exactly that in this instance with the devil in the wilderness and showed us as men of God what to do when faced with situations that are not made for your favour.

What I really love about this is the reality and relatability of it for us as men, it shows us that no one is invincible, no one is exempt from the temptations of life. Everyone gets tempted and it doesn't make it a character flaw, but your response does.

Now we know this, we can speak from a more real level; pressure is going to come, but your character is tested when you are tempted. Temptation just proves what is on your insides, like what have you built in there, what morals do you have, what have you been reading, what have you been consuming, what foundations do you have, these questions will all be answered when you are tested. In order for your character to be proven, tests need to come!

Every day that you go into the world you are proving your character, if we want to be realistic the wilderness for us in this generation as men of God is the world, university for some of us, even work for some of us. Wherever it is, think of it as your wilderness where your character is going to be tested. I believe if we approached life with this mentality, along with the keys to character, we would display better character in our lives. We love a challenge as men, we love proving ourselves, so if you know the world isn't designed to help you display Godly character then you can prove it wrong. Use your male ego and pride for the right reasons here.

WHAT IS A MAN?

PRESSURE PROVES CHARACTER

Pressure can prove what is inside of you, not just being in the environment, but the pressure of the environment on you, the environment trying to influence you. We have the example of this below in Matthew 4:3-10 where Jesus answered a series of questions, given some alternatives, given options, almost a way out of walking in the Word of God and His response is quite astounding. Let's read and then we will assess:

> *"The tempter came to him and said, "If you are the Son of God, tell these stones to become bread." Jesus answered, "It is written: 'Man shall not live on bread alone, but on every word that comes from the mouth of God." Then the devil took him to the holy city and had him stand on the highest point of the temple. "If you are the Son of God," he said, "throw yourself down. For it is written: "'He will command his angels concerning you, and they will lift you up in their hands, so that you will not strike your foot against a stone.'" Jesus answered him, "It is also written: 'Do not put the Lord your God to the test.'" Again, the devil took him to a very high mountain and showed him all the kingdoms of the world and their splendour. "All this I will give you," he said, "if you will bow down and worship me." Jesus said to him, "Away from me, Satan! For it is written: 'Worship the Lord your God and serve him only.'"" Matthew 4:3-10 NIV*

The enemy tried to offer Jesus what He already possessed inside, but if Jesus didn't know the Word, He would have been drawn to that and fooled by it. But as we see from here Jesus came back with the best response that was possible, He came back with the Word, so we can see what was inside of Him. Jesus was fully God and fully man, and His character was

WHAT IS A MAN?

therefore shaped by the Word. So He just responded with what He knew.

WHAT YOU MEDITATE ON WILL MANIFEST!

Sometimes this may happen to you, you may be offered a promotion if you just do this one immoral thing, you may be offered unlimited money, only if you just start selling drugs, you may be offered brotherhood if you just join this gang, whatever it is, it is not worth you giving in to. Character must be submitted to God, so that when the time comes and you are pressured, the things of God can respond.

Isn't it interesting that the only thing Jesus mentioned was the Word, like He didn't say anything else. His character was that submitted that He wasn't even moved by the temptation, He wasn't moved by the offers, He just stood firm in His character and His place. This is because when you submit to God, your automatic response is to resist the devil and when you do this, he can only do one thing which is flee.

"Submit yourselves, then, to God. Resist the devil, and he will flee from you." James 4:7 NIV

SUBMITTING TO GOD MEANS RESISTING THE DEVIL!

This is a key in your life, submit fully to God and make sure that every action follows that and then also become one with the Word. How do you do this? You do this by making sure you spend time reading the Word, studying the Word, and also looking at how the Word can shape you, mould you and develop you.

WHAT IS A MAN?

THE WORD PASSES EVERY TEST

The question would be for many of us, is **"If the Word passes every test then why you would fail?"** This is a question that many of us struggle with, why is it that every day we fail and succumb to temptation, why is it every day we don't walk in the right character and most of the time this is because we have missed the foundation of character which is the Word of God. We have refused to measure ourselves by the standard of the Word, because we see it as an ideal rather than a yardstick, we see it as a guideline rather than a criterion. The Word is there to help you to overcome the temptations of this life. There is nothing you face today that hasn't been answered in the Word and this is what you will find out if you are submitted to God as a basis but are also one with the Word of God. The Word of God needs to ooze out of you, it needs to be coming off your lips on a regular basis, it needs to be the foundation of you, the foundation of your character!

Choose God and choose to become one with the Word and you will see these character keys begin to become easier!

RECAP

- Being submitted to the Word and being one with the Word is foundation of character!
- Your character will be tested, and the test will prove what is inside of you!
- The only way to guarantee your character will pass every test and temptation is by responding with the Word!
- Temptation doesn't make you a sinner, it makes you human!
- What you meditated on will manifest so meditate on the Word

WHAT IS A MAN?

Space for reflection

When reading this chapter and reviewing your life is there anything that you have noticed that stands out to you? Is there anything that has helped answer any questions you had about manhood? Use the space below to note anything down that you need to.

WHAT IS A MAN?

HEART CHECK

When we look at character in this book it is all based upon the Word and tailored to men as well; for the most part as we have discussed earlier men are not walking in Good character which is also linked to them not walking in the purpose God has for their life. As we looked at the Word being the foundation for character in the introduction, I believe it is important that we look at our heart next.

There are many ways to look at the heart of a man and to assess it, but I think it is important that we discuss this because many people have been getting away with having hearts for themselves and for their own gain, but we are going to stop that in its tracks today. We all know that men are called to lead, we are called to be the heads of houses, we are called to be fathers, we are called to be leaders, but it is important that the posture of your heart is in the right place.

Many leaders don't have the right character and many men also don't have the right character, and that is because their heart is in the wrong place. When we look at the example of Jesus, we see that He had a heart for others and as a man this is the example that we need to take; wherever you are you need to make sure that you are reflecting the heart of God because it is a character key that is necessary for life.

We have seen many leaders fall, many leaders be despised, and many leaders lose long term impact due to their lack of heart for people. You are not ready to lead anyone if your heart is in the wrong place, don't think you are walking in character if your heart is not in the right place. What we are doing in this chapter is a quick heart check.

A man with the heart of Christ, displays the correct character. Having the heart of Christ is stepping up from being submitted to the Word because it is ensuring that your heart is transformed

WHAT IS A MAN?

and moulded by the Word to inform your character and your actions. As a leader this would mean you wouldn't lead like we have seen many leaders lead in recent times or even in the past, but you would lead like Jesus; let's look at the Word and see what this looks like practically.

"As Jesus was walking beside the Sea of Galilee, he saw two brothers, Simon called Peter and his brother Andrew. They were casting a net into the lake, for they were fishermen. "Come, follow me," Jesus said, "and I will send you out to fish for people." At once they left their nets and followed him. Going on from there, he saw two other brothers, James son of Zebedee and his brother John. They were in a boat with their father Zebedee, preparing their nets. Jesus called them, and immediately they left the boat and their father and followed him." Matthew 4:18-22 NIV

IT ALL STARTS WITH THE HEART!

"Your motives inform your methods" what does this phrase mean? This is something that I noticed when studying Jesus and His character, Jesus' motivation was to serve other people and to push them to purpose. We look at this first because as I have stated; submission and service are two things that men cannot really get to grips with and this is something that God showed me that was especially important when looking at character is, what is the posture of one's heart and what are their motives. In order to walk in the right character as a man you need to have the right heart!

"Then He said to them, "Follow Me, and I will make you fishers of men."" Matthew 4:19 NKJV

We see this lived out from Jesus specifically in this passage here; Jesus said, **"follow me so I can make you"** and this is important for character because He was telling these disciples He was going to lead them, but we see here that His posture and

WHAT IS A MAN?

positioning are in a different place to where we see normal leaders nowadays. Jesus wanted to make them something, most leaders recruit so that people can make them something. Many men have become so used to this world's view of leadership and being a man that is about manipulating people into doing things for them and using people for their own gain, that hearing something like this is going to be a foreign concept for some of them.

What we are discussing here is going to be counter cultural, this is a style of man or character who lives and leads from a heart posture of service, **a humble heart**! You can't be a man of character if your heart isn't humble, this is what differentiated Jesus as a leader and all of the other leaders of that time and even still those now. Jesus' life was informed by His character which was informed by a humble heart and His heart was moulded by the Word!

WHAT IS YOUR HEART LIKE?

This is something we have to ask ourselves on a regular basis, we have to be able to assess, we have to be held accountable for where our heart is because the scripture even tells us to guard our hearts because out of that flows everything. God knew what He was doing when He inspired that to be written because men lack character because their heart has been influenced by contemporary culture, greed, or power. The culture shapes their character into doing whatever it takes for power, money, control; which leaves us with a world where a lot of men look nothing like what God intended. Yeah they're rich and skilful, but that is not the sum total of what God meant when He talked about us being a living breathing reflection of Him.

"Above all else, guard your heart, for everything you do flows from it." Proverbs 4:23 NIV

WHAT IS A MAN?

I read a book by Dr Matthew Stevenson called **"Strange Fire"** and it was such a perfectly timed book because it really came at a season where God was teaching me about character and motives. This book really allowed me to reflect and honestly check my heart, what was informing what I was doing? What was my why? Like where was my heart at concerning the things in my life? Did I want to do things for the right reasons? Did I want things for the right reasons, or had I got caught up in the ways of society where everything is for personal gain? This is how self-aware we have to be because your heart informs your character, you can't have a good character if you don't have a good heart.

LET ME LEAD

The aspect of leadership is different when your heart is humble and a heart of service. God doesn't want you to lead from a place of power but instead from a place of service. He was the leader, but He led by service. When I say your motive informs your methods, I mean literally that the method of leadership, of love, of living, of learning is all informed by your motives.

If you have a heart of service you are able to lead from a pure place, if you have a heart of love you are able to love from a pure place, if you have a heart of humility you are able to learn from a pure place and if you have a heart of sacrifice you are able to live from a pure place. Jesus came to this earth with a great heart of humility and service.

"just as the Son of Man did not come to be served, but to serve, and to give his life as a ransom for many."" **Matthew 20:28 NIV**

Many of us want to lead for our own success and this shows a real heart defect, this is why Jesus shows us something called *leadership discipleship*! This is the perfect combination of having character as a man and how it would inform leadership. Leadership as we know it is not personal, because the leader's

WHAT IS A MAN?

emphasis is on leading a team for His success, not necessarily for theirs. Jesus' heart was for the success and the growth of His disciples, when you have a heart of service you don't just lead your team you disciple them. The biggest way to check your heart and reason for wanting leadership is how you actually deal with the people that God gives you to lead.

Discipleship is a personal way of leadership, because when you disciple somebody you care about more than their performance in your team, but instead you care about their life, purpose, wellbeing, heart, and this is what Jesus shows us. His heart was to disciple others, and by His motives being to build them, you can see that He was wanting to lead them to a place of success, from a place of service.

HEART POSTURE

We have been using the example of leadership because it is a position men are often found in, and one of the biggest places they fall due to lack of character. I hope that through reading this you begin to understand that something very key:

YOUR POSITION DOESN'T NECESSARILY AFFIRM OR CONFIRM YOUR POSTURE!

We see many leaders who don't have the right heart posture but that doesn't mean that it is right, this trend is what we are trying to stop. Men of positions need to also be men of the right heart posture! We are going to look at the four postures of your heart and how they can work in informing your character as a man. It's vital to assess yourself based on these heart postures honestly, and then have the answers to be able to move forward from this!

WHAT IS A MAN?

1. A Heart of Love

"And walk in love, as Christ also has loved us and given Himself for us, an offering and a sacrifice to God for a sweet-smelling aroma." Ephesians 5:2 NKJV

"Let love be the foundation and motivation of everything that you do!" This is something that is so key for you in your life, your heart posture is something that dictates your movements, actions and character. A heart of love isn't just a heart that loves but a heart of love is a heart that displays love from a place of overflow because of the love of God in your heart.

Men are usually consumed by lust, so therefore our character is shaped and moulded by the lust in our hearts. Many of us are exhibiting bad traits, walking in bad character because we lust after things; we lust after power, we lust after positions, we lust after possessions and this therefore informs the way we behave, it leads to manipulation, anger, and coercion.

Check where your heart is when it comes to love, is your heart filled with love? Am I doing this based on love? Am I thinking from a position of love?

You can walk with a heart of love by making sure you are consumed by the love of God in such a way that shapes your character. Meditate on the Word of God, read His Word to hear and see His love for you and communicate with Him, and allow Him to speak to you. Let God tell you how He feels about you and this will allow you to begin to grow and be shaped by God's Word and His love.

WHAT IS A MAN?

2. A Heart of Service

"not looking to your own interests but each of you to the interests of the others." Philippians 2:4 NIV

A heart of service is a heart that desires the betterment of others rather than just self. We see from Jesus that He had a heart of service because He wanted to serve others rather than being served, He also mentioned that it is better to give than receive, in Acts 20:35.

This heart posture is that is counter cultural, especially for men, because we live in a society that has placed men on a pedestal where we are worshipped, served and loved like kings but we aren't ever taught to serve. This societal construct is what leads to many men having a struggle with the heart of service. Everyone wants to be on top, to lead, to have the power but is there not power in choosing to serve and building others? This is a question you should really think about. **"Who is more powerful, the person who is in charge or the person who empowers the person who's in charge?"**

I read once in a leadership book when studying my degree that, **"A leader cannot lead without followers"**. Followers are people with the heart of service, so they are the ones with the power because they enable and empower the leader to lead by choosing to follow. Something to look at it is, how can you be a leader if you first haven't been led? The best leaders we have seen to date, holistically have been; **servant leaders** (people who lead from a place of service).

How do you develop a heart of service? I believe this is a perspective and paradigm shift that needs to happen, Romans 12:2 talks about renewing the mind and this is a key in developing a heart of service. You need to see service differently to the way you have seen it before; you need to begin to think of others more, you need to begin to look at Jesus and the opinions that God has of those who are servants. Begin to pray for God to give you the heart of service! This scripture should help you to understand God's view on those who choose the heart of service!

"But they kept quiet because on the way they had argued about who was the greatest. Sitting down, Jesus called the Twelve and said, "Anyone who wants to be first must be the very last, and the servant of all.""" Mark 9:34-35 NIV

3. A Heart of Humility

"Humble yourselves before the Lord, and he will lift you up." James 4:10 NIV

Character has to be based on the premise of humility, if your heart is not humble God promises you one thing, you will fall, because pride comes before a fall. When you are humble you understand that God is the superior power, He is in control, the author and finisher, the one who gives you the ability to have good character.

Many men love the phrase **"self-made"** which is one of the most prideful statements that can ever be made, because it promotes a brash and toxic mentality that gives people the impression that no one else contributed to the journey of their success. The **"I did all this"** mentality is something that causes many of us to fall tragically to our demise! The refusal to humble yourself before God is what causes your leadership to fail, your life to fail and a lot of the time the way you love to fail.

Pride causes us to think we know everything and that we don't need help. We struggle to progress because we struggle to seek help, direction, and information from others, instead we are **comfortable in our dysfunction.** Some of us would rather be a failure and have control, than be a success and be humble.

WHAT IS A MAN?

Humility is **"the ability to think of oneself soberly"**, this means that you don't think you are better than you are, but you also don't think you are worse than you are. The best place to learn humility is from Jesus because God gives us a promise for humility, Jesus was God and still humbled Himself. Humble yourself before God and He lifts you up, when you have a heart of humility the weight of lifting is off of yourself. You don't have to act, to manipulate, to scheme, or play the system because it is God who lifts you up.

4. A Heart of Sacrifice

"Greater love has no one than this: to lay down one's life for one's friends." John 15:13 NIV

Sacrifice is the final key heart posture we are going to look at. Are you willing to give things up for others? Are you willing to give yourself to others? Are you willing to give your time for others? Are you willing to be inconvenienced for others? This may be something that is an anomaly to some of us men because we are used to women who sacrifice for us, but if we think about it, we need this heart posture to have good character.

We sometimes need to sacrifice our opinions for the sake of relationships, sometimes we have to sacrifice our time for the sake of building someone's confidence, sometimes we also have to sacrifice by going the extra mile to show our love to someone. This is all part of character and building a character that is reflective of Jesus, but it all starts with the heart. Does your heart see sacrifice as an honour? Or does it see sacrifice as a burden? Jesus saw sacrificing His life as an honour, He saw sacrificing His public reputation as an honour in serving the kingdom.

WHAT IS A MAN?

RECAP

- Motives inform your methods
- It all starts with the heart
- Check the posture of your heart before you do anything
- Your character is shaped by the posture of your heart
- You need a heart of love, a heart of service, a heart of humility and a heart of sacrifice to be able to walk in Godly character

WHAT IS A MAN?

Space for reflection

When reading this chapter and reviewing your life is there anything that you have noticed that stands out to you? Is there anything that has helped answer any questions you had about manhood? Use the space below to note anything down that you need to.

WHAT IS A MAN?

THE HIGHER STANDARD

So far we have looked at the foundation of character, we have looked at the heart posture of character and now we are going to look at some of the character keys, the first one being the higher standard, GRACE!

WALK WITH GRACE, WALK IN GRACE AND WALK BY GRACE!

DEFINING GRACE

- Unmerited favour
- The free opportunity to live a righteous life!
- Understanding that Grace was paid for you to walk in
- Grace is a Higher Standard

The scripture that we are going to look at is Matthew 5:20-48, where Jesus describes the higher standard to us as men. Jesus brings us a new standard that we should live by. He tells us what the law used to be based on, but He also showed us what Grace requires and gives us the power to do. Not only did Jesus talk about this but instead He walked in this new standard of character.

Does law make good character or does law modify and control behaviour? This is something that Jesus wanted to address,. so that those who read it can now see this standard and walk in character that is on a new level. What we need to come to as men is a standard where we don't flirt with danger!

WHAT IS A MAN?

"For I tell you that unless your righteousness surpasses that of the Pharisees and the teachers of the law, you will certainly not enter the kingdom of heaven. "You have heard that it was said to the people long ago, 'You shall not murder, and anyone who murders will be subject to judgment.' But I tell you that anyone who is angry with a brother or sister will be subject to judgment. Again, anyone who says to a brother or sister, 'Raca,' is answerable to the court. And anyone who says, 'You fool!' will be in danger of the fire of hell. "Therefore, if you are offering your gift at the altar and there remember that your brother or sister has something against you, leave your gift there in front of the altar. First go and be reconciled to them; then come and offer your gift. "Settle matters quickly with your adversary who is taking you to court. Do it while you are still together on the way, or your adversary may hand you over to the judge, and the judge may hand you over to the officer, and you may be thrown into prison. Truly I tell you, you will not get out until you have paid the last penny. "You have heard that it was said, 'You shall not commit adultery.' But I tell you that anyone who looks at a woman lustfully has already committed adultery with her in his heart. If your right eye causes you to stumble, gouge it out and throw it away. It is better for you to lose one part of your body than for your whole body to be thrown into hell. And if your right hand causes you to stumble, cut it off and throw it away. It is better for you to lose one part of your body than for your whole body to go into hell. "It has been said, 'Anyone who divorces his wife must give her a certificate of divorce.' But I tell you that anyone who divorces his wife, except for sexual immorality, makes her the victim of adultery, and anyone who marries a divorced woman commits adultery.

WHAT IS A MAN?

> "Again, you have heard that it was said to the people long ago, 'Do not break your oath, but fulfil to the Lord the vows you have made.' But I tell you, do not swear an oath at all: either by heaven, for it is God's throne; or by the earth, for it is his footstool; or by Jerusalem, for it is the city of the Great King. And do not swear by your head, for you cannot make even one hair white or black. All you need to say is simply 'Yes' or 'No'; anything beyond this comes from the evil one. "You have heard that it was said, 'Eye for eye, and tooth for tooth.' But I tell you, do not resist an evil person. If anyone slaps you on the right cheek, turn to them the other cheek also. And if anyone wants to sue you and take your shirt, hand over your coat as well. If anyone forces you to go one mile, go with them two miles. Give to the one who asks you, and do not turn away from the one who wants to borrow from you. "You have heard that it was said, 'Love your neighbour and hate your enemy.' But I tell you, love your enemies and pray for those who persecute you, that you may be children of your Father in heaven. He causes his sun to rise on the evil and the good and sends rain on the righteous and the unrighteous. If you love those who love you, what reward will you get? Are not even the tax collectors doing that? And if you greet only your own people, what are you doing more than others? Do not even pagans do that? Be perfect, therefore, as your heavenly Father is perfect."
> *Matthew 5:20-48 NIV*

WHAT IS A MAN?

JESUS HAS CHANGED THE BAR!

This new bar allows us to walk in the Grace of God, it is the blueprint for character! If there's a problem with the fruits of your character then it is important to check the root, as the root is the standard at which you hold yourself to. Most of our roots aren't right because they are usually informed by the standards of society, which promotes a life of **"as long as you don't get caught you should be fine"**. Society doesn't have any concern for the roots, it doesn't even address the root, it just punishes the fruit! If you want to walk in character you need to be concerned about the roots, if they're wrong then put down new ones based upon the scriptures.

Jesus wants us to walk righteously, He wants us to walk in the character of God, this is why He brings this new standard. As a man of God there has to be a noticeable difference between you and the world, you can't operate like the world, or live like the world, you have to be different. Being able to keep the law is not a compliment to your character, but instead being able to walk by the higher standard is what defines your character.

GOD'S GRACE ENABLES YOU TO WALK IN GRACE!

We have found that Grace is the free opportunity to live a righteous life, the unmerited favour of God, that was brought about by the death of Jesus for your sins and iniquities. This is what enables you to walk in the Grace that is the Higher Standard. What God already did, enables you to walk in what standard is required of you as a believer through the price of Grace paid. You aren't meant to do it alone. You need the Grace of God to walk in Grace!

When you walk in Grace, you don't actually ever come into problems with the law because your character is exemplary, it is of a different level and category to those who come into problems with the law... Grace is free for everyone! Better

WHAT IS A MAN?

character is what separates you from the average man. Jesus was not your average man and He has given us the blueprint for this life of character, which we will look into after this.

Your character should be so distinguished that people should be attracted to it; they should want to know what caused you to exhibit behaviour like this. What is your source of restraint? What is your source of peace? Who waters your roots? What gives you the power to stay strong? What enables you to walk out this higher standard?

MAKING IT PRACTICAL

Something that we need to look at is how does the scripture make Grace > Law practical to us today and how can we do it in this generation... let's have a look at some of the examples:

"You shall not Murder" is Law – "you shall not even get angry" is Grace

"You shall not commit adultery" is law – "you shall not look at a woman lustfully" is Grace.

"You shall not break an oath" is law – "you shouldn't even swear oaths" is Grace

What we see here is 3 examples of the new standard that Jesus is talking about, and we can even make it more practical in our lives today as men.

There are things that we struggle with that we need to cut at the root. Let's look at things like arrogance, masturbation, manipulation, pride, we could go on, but these things need to be cut at the root. Some of us need to check our perspective on these things, we have chosen to flirt with danger and live by the standard of the Word. If we want to be the man God has called us to be, we need to choose today to live by the higher standard.

WHAT IS A MAN?

It starts with knowing what that standard is, knowing the benefits, knowing the purpose, and desiring to walk in it. If you say you want to be the best man you can be, then you should want to walk in the higher standard.

Desire to have better character! Desire to be an example and a reflection of Jesus on earth and you cannot do that if you don't have a character that walks in Grace.

Even begin to ask yourself, **"Is there anything that I am currently walking in that promotes the normal standard of life?"** Am I content with living being just like everyone else? Do I want more? Am I willing to make the necessary adjustments to live by a higher standard? Am I ready to uproot the norms? Assess yourself honestly because if you want to walk in the character God intended for men, you need to be able assess your perspective, paradigm, and you need to assess your current roots.

The key in all of this is making sure that you reflect your Father in heaven as it states in verse 48:

"Be perfect, therefore, as your heavenly Father is perfect."

Let the standard of your character be God, let the living example of your character be Jesus and let the potter and refiner of your character be the Holy Spirit!

As a man, you are a target, even more so as a man of God, you are a target of the enemy's plots and schemes so you need to ensure that the character you are exhibiting is that of Christ and is refined by the Holy Spirit because you will pass every test when your standard is Grace and the Word. Make sure that you adapt the higher standard because the higher you go in terms of influence and notoriety the more important living by Grace is!

WHAT IS A MAN?

RECAP

- Grace is a higher standard of living, it's a new bar
- Grace deals with the root to prevent the display of bad fruit
- The same Grace that saved you is the same Grace that can sustain you
- Your character should be attractive to others
- You can walk in perfection with the refining of the Holy Spirit, the example of Jesus and the Grace of God

WHAT IS A MAN?

Space for reflection

When reading this chapter and reviewing your life is there anything that you have noticed that stands out to you? Is there anything that has helped answer any questions you had about manhood? Use the space below to note anything down that you need to.

WHAT IS A MAN?

FIX YOUR FOCUS

Something that we are going to look at in this chapter, is focus! A man of character has to be a man of focus! Many of us in this life have our focus on the wrong things; like getting money by any means and end up doing things that are unlawful which could cause them to leave kids with absent fathers due to death, or jail.

It is important that we understand how important focus is to shaping character, what you focus on shapes the things you will do but also the character you begin to exhibit. As a man our focus affects so many people; whether it's a son, a younger sibling, a nephew, a wife, a daughter, what you focus on is going to have effects on other people and their lives. Some men even focus on sex, so instead of building an intimate relationship and having a covenant of marriage that creates the safe and correct environment for sex to happen, they go out and manipulate, lie, and even pay to fill the desire for sex. The effects this has on women, is that their purity is taken, their self-worth is decreased, and they could even end up pregnant.

YOUR FOCUS AFFECTS NOT ONLY YOU BUT THOSE AROUND YOU!

Every season requires a different focus; when you're a young single man your main priority isn't going to be a wife and kids, but it may be university, relationship with God, walking in gifting and establishing the foundations of a career. For a married man, your priorities are your relationship with God, your wife, providing for your family, walking in God's call for your life and leading and carrying vision for your family.

There is one focus that will always remain, no matter what season of life you are in, you need to start with the right foundation.

A MAN OF CHARACTER IS A MAN OF FOCUS!

WHAT IS A MAN?

DEFINING FOCUS

- The main or central point of something, especially of attention or interest
- To direct attention toward something or someone
- To adjust something in order to see more clearly

We are going to break down each one of these and show how they relate to your main focus for life and character which is the ***kingdom of God***!

"But seek first his kingdom and his righteousness, and all these things will be given to you as well." Matthew 6:33 NIV

WHAT IS THE KINGDOM?

"The spiritual reign or authority of God!"

This is the dictionary definition of the kingdom, but I wanted to break it down for you into 2 parts so you can understand the kingdom in depth.

The King: God
His domain/ dominion: Heaven

Having this is as your focus, means that your character is shaped by the King to reflect His domain on Earth. This is the instruction we have from Jesus in this scripture.

Let's look at the 3 different definitions of focus and how they shape your character, how they help you to walk in the character you are called to!

WHAT IS A MAN?

1. The main or central point of something, especially of attention or interest

The world that we live in feeds us with so many external influences that it is sometimes hard for us to focus on one thing, but if you want to walk in character, your priority needs to be making God the centre of your life. God needs to be your focus and being like Him, you need to be paying special attention to God through His Word, through prayer so that you can learn more about Him, so you can become more and more like Him in nature and in character.

When we look at Jesus, we see a perfect example here, because He walked the earth saying, **"I only do the will of my Father."** Jesus lived His life focused on one thing and that was pleasing the King and bringing heaven to Earth. His whole life mission and aim was to reflect God on Earth and do what God wanted Him to do. What you begin to find is that when you seek the king you begin to know more about what He wants; you begin to walk in your divinity and then that causes you to walk righteously. It all starts with the king, making Him your focus! He has to be the main priority in your life because that is what informs your righteous character.

Make the decision today to make God your central focus!

"For I have come down from heaven not to do my will but to do the will of him who sent me." John 6:38 NIV

2. To direct attention toward something or someone

Another aspect of focusing on God means that you aim to bring as much attention to Him as possible. This reflective in your character because it means that you think outside of yourself when reflecting character, like discussed earlier in the chapter, you are aware that your character has effects on other people, so

WHAT IS A MAN?

it is vital that you exhibit the character that directs attention towards God and not away from Him.

Many men don't bring people to Christ because they look just like the people they are trying to save, and I am not talking about clothes. Everything about you must point in the direction of God, whether that be your life, your success, your righteousness, or in the way you speak, you have to be focused on establishing the kingdom of God on this earth.

Take the focus off of yourself and shift it to God. Your character should be the navigation system towards God for others, so everything about you should bring them closer to Him. What we begin to see is that our character becomes one so focused on God and establishing the kingdom on earth that any attention we get, is for His Glory and we begin to seek every opportunity to display God to others in our character. We have to remember that we are sometimes the only Jesus that people see, so we need to be focused on God and bringing the attention to Him!

Bring the attention to God by your conduct, the way you operate at work, the way you operate in school, the way you operate in uni, the way you operate in your clubs. Make sure that people are getting a representation of a different type of character through your focus on directing attention to Him.

3. To adjust something in order to see more clearly

This final type of focus is key for us as men in particular because many people have got a blurry image of what being a man means. This is further perpetuated because they see infidelity in the church, lying, or sex before marriage, so it is hard to clearly tell the difference.

Our role is to show them the difference, to make the picture of God and character clearer for them. You are called to shed light on the kingdom of God and its importance to every human being

WHAT IS A MAN?

by your lifestyle, and by knowing the Word more. You are supposed to be the magnifying glass for people to be able to see what God truly looks like. More importantly; what a man of God truly looks like.

The truest way to do this is by zooming in on God more for yourself, knowing God intimately, being shown revelation of the true nature of God, so that you are able to show others from a position of revelation rather than rhetoric. When you look at cameras, in order to see something more clearly or in more detail they focus in on the thing. This is what we are called to do with God, we are called to focus in on Him to such point where we begin to see the details and the intricacies of Him. As we do this, we begin to see more about ourselves and He can shape us, build us.

The reason that people have a distorted view of character is because their focus is off, they don't know enough about God or His character to know character and how to walk in it, therefore God looks distant to them and so does good character. This is why this scripture is vital because it teaches us that our main focus needs to be God, then His dominion/ domain and that will lead us to righteousness which will cause us to inherit all things; including great character. Things don't just have to mean money, or material things but they can be characteristics, spiritual gifts and if we'd just fix our focus, we will realise that walking in good character is a part of focusing on God as a priority.

Could it be that God tells you to seek Him first because until you focus in on Him and see Him more clearly you can't recognise everything that comes with the kingdom? If you have no focus you continue to live a blurred and character flawed life!

WHEN YOU REALISE THAT GOD IS THE MAIN FOCUS OF YOUR LIFE, YOU BEGIN TO GAIN ACCESS TO EVERYTHING THAT HE HAS ACCESS TO!

WHAT IS A MAN?

RECAP

- Character is a result of what you focus on, so a man of character has to be a man focused on God and reflecting the kingdom through righteousness
- Fix your focus on seeing God more clearly
- In everything you do draw the attention and focus to God
- What you focus on affects other people
- You can't be focused on pleasing God and display unrighteous character because the more you get to know God you get a clearer picture of what character you are called to walk in
- Character is one of the things that you receive when you seek God first

WHAT IS A MAN?

Space for reflection

When reading this chapter and reviewing your life is there anything that you have noticed that stands out to you? Is there anything that has helped answer any questions you had about manhood? Use the space below to note anything down that you need to.

WHAT IS A MAN?

INTEGRITY

Character is key and so are the keys to Godly character! One of them that is paramount is integrity, which seems to be something that is missing in this world a lot. Those of the world operate contrary to integrity because they want what they want, and they don't care how they get it or who they become in the process. If integrity is lacking in this earth, then it is important that you don't take your cues from the earth in terms of character, integrity, and morals.

DEFINING INTEGRITY

Integrity is defined by Oxford languages as two things.
- The quality of being honest and having strong moral principles.
- The state of being whole and undivided.

Some synonyms are:
- Honesty
- Uprightness
- Honour
- Unity
- Wholeness
- Coherence

What I love about this Word is that it is multidimensional, but it is a standard that challenges our humanity as well. Some of the words that you are seeing here are words you are familiar with but may choose not to live by while being influenced by secular culture.

A MAN OF CHARACTER IS A MAN OF INTEGRITY!

As a man of character it is important to be led by the Word and the Word points out that integrity is key. We are going to take a look at integrity and how that looks practically for you as a man so that you are able to walk in the character God expects and Jesus exemplified.

"For in the same way you judge others, you will be judged, and with the measure you use, it will be measured to you. "Why do you look at the speck of sawdust in your brother's eye and pay no attention to the plank in your own eye? How can you say to your brother, 'Let me take the speck out of your eye,' when all the time there is a plank in your own eye? You hypocrite first take the plank out of your own eye, and then you will see clearly to remove the speck from your brother's eye. "Do not give dogs what is sacred; do not throw your pearls to pigs. If you do, they may trample them under their feet, and turn and tear you to pieces." Matthew 7:2-6 NIV

Jesus explains something profound when He begins to talk about judgement of others, and it conflicts with our humanity because as human beings our normal nature is not to be integral but instead to lie, cheat and manipulate. Now as believers we have the conflict of following the standards and constructs of society or do we operate differently.

Every day on social media we are presented with many influences; judging others, criticising others, having double standards for men and women, not being self-aware, or being hypocritical. We have a lot of things that can help us to not walk in integrity so how do we follow what Jesus is saying when we are seeing this so often? Jesus is presenting a blueprint for something different, something that displays the character of God to the world and as we know God is a god of integrity like it says in Numbers 23:19!

"God is not human, that he should lie, not a human being, that he should change his mind. Does he speak and then not act? Does he promise and not fulfil?" Numbers 23:19 NIV

WHAT IS A MAN?

There are some very important signposts that these scriptures give us that can help us to walk in integrity and understand integrity in more depth.

1. One Standard

Something I want to identify here is that the double standard between men and women is so rife in the world. Women are expected to uphold a certain standard and are judged on a different measuring stick than that of men, and that is what men have put in place, because of pride and arrogance and the power that we have in this world.

We are going to dispel that myth and bring integrity to you as a man because you are going to be different, you are going to have integrity. We are called to live by one standard and that standard is the Word; integrity is what you are called to! One standard means being undivided and stable. Something we know in this society is that the standard changes all the time, so it causes us to be unstable and that is the reason why we have to walk on the Word as our standard.

"Such a person is double-minded and unstable in all they do." James 1:8 NIV

Now the funny thing about this is that if I asked you **"How many of you want to be unstable?"** you would question my sanity but that is exactly what you are every day if you do not walk in integrity. A man who hasn't got integrity assumes that they have the right to hold someone else to a different standard to them, they believe they have the right to judge others as if they are God. The more you are judging others by a different standard to you is the more prideful you are!

WHAT IS A MAN?

So shoutout for all men;

WE HAVE BEEN PRIDEFUL BY HAVING DOUBLE STANDARDS WHEN IT COMES TO CONDUCT AND CHARACTER OF MEN AND WOMEN!

Something that God promises us is that if we judge others by a different measuring stick then we will be judged by that standard as well, so let's put it in context; Men judge any woman that sleeps with more than a few men as a "hoe" but if that were a man, they would say that he is a real man, a top dog. God wants to just bring us to one standard and that is the Word; the Word says you shouldn't commit adultery or even lust after a woman so that is the standard, for both men and women, anything else is someone trying to walk outside of God's standards.

Integrity promotes unity. As the scripture says don't talk about the speck in someone else's eyes when you have a plank in yours. This is vital because a man of integrity lives by the Word, measures by the Word, and aims to be like Jesus. Any comments to anyone else are from a place of promoting unity within the kingdom and to maintain the standard rather than to judge by another standard. There is a balance that is necessary because a man of integrity must be honest, which means if he sees that someone is not operating within the standard of the Word they will go to their brother and tell them, but they would not be walking contrary to the Word and telling people to walk in the Word because that is hypocrisy.

DON'T BE A HYPOCRITE!

Being a man of integrity is all about being whole and undivided. Be honourable, bring unity, don't bring division by having double standard, instead bring everyone to the common standard of the Word and do it in love!

WHAT IS A MAN?

"So, Christ himself gave the apostles, the prophets, the evangelists, the pastors, and teachers, to equip his people for works of service, so that the body of Christ may be built up until we all reach unity in the faith and in the knowledge of the Son of God and become mature, attaining to the whole measure of the fullness of Christ. Then we will no longer be infants, tossed back and forth by the waves, and blown here and there by every wind of teaching and by the cunning and craftiness of people in their deceitful scheming. Instead, speaking the truth in love, we will grow to become in every respect the mature body of him who is the head, that is, Christ. From him the whole body, joined and held together by every supporting ligament, grows, and builds itself up in love, as each part does its work."
Ephesians 4:11-16 NIV

As a man of integrity, you need to be seen as someone who reflects the character of God! Hypocrites measure people by a standard they are not prepared to live by; but when you use the Word as the standard you have integrity because you are bringing more people to reflect God in a better light!

2. Fix YOU First!

This aspect of integrity is something that as humans we seem to avoid, like we want to fix others, but we don't want to fix ourselves. We seem to have this unbelievable desire to tell other people where they are going wrong and it isn't just in church, but it is across life, we love to feel like we have the power to tell someone they aren't quite doing something right. What I present to you today is that integrity has the mentality of fixing you first before you start judging others and trying to fix them.

In order to be integral, you have to be ready to self-reflect, and self-analyse/ assess honestly, because it is needed. How do you improve if you haven't accepted that there is a log in your own eye? How do you even see the speck in someone's eye if you haven't removed the plank in yours? What gives you the right or

WHAT IS A MAN?

authority to judge people if you aren't willing to meet that standard? One of the best forms of helping others is by being and doing; as a man of integrity this is something that you need to be able to walk in, as a norm.

If you notice a problem in your own life, the focus should be on becoming whole within yourself before commenting on the failures of others. Integrity is all about being whole, begin coherent and being honest, but many of us fail to do anything about our own shortcomings. When we talk about wholeness, that isn't just unified wholeness in the kingdom of God but in yourself. Be a person who is able to assess themselves and fix the broken areas of their life or allow themselves to be fixed! Jesus is explaining a type of lifestyle that promotes coherence and wholeness. If you haven't got yourself together what place do you have to try and fix others.

BROKEN PEOPLE CANNOT FIX EACH OTHER, THEY CAN ONLY HELP EACH OTHER TO BECOME MORE BROKEN!

One of the keys to integrity and fixing yourself first is to be honest. Be honest with where you are at, be honest with what you are struggling with and be accountable. Many of us as men struggle to accept our struggle, we struggle to accept help or even ask for it. I believe that the rise in men and mental health stems from the fact that we go through things, we struggle but we don't seek help, we believe too much in our masculinity and then the problems begin to compound!

FIND SOMEONE, WHO CAN HELP YOU! MANY OF US ARE STUNTING OUR OWN GROWTH BECAUSE WE HAVE NO INTEGRITY!

WHAT IS A MAN?

RECAP

- Match your life to the Word and encourage others to do so because this promotes unity
- Be so focused on reflecting God that your light causes others to want it
- Be honest in your assessment of yourself and be accountable and be whole
- Pride is something that stops us from walking in integrity as men who have double standards.
- A man of integrity talks from a place of being and doing!

WHAT IS A MAN?

Space for reflection

When reading this chapter and reviewing your life is there anything that you have noticed that stands out to you? Is there anything that has helped answer any questions you had about manhood? Use the space below to note anything down that you need to.

WHAT IS A MAN?

STRENGTH, NO WEAKNESS

Did you hear about the little boy from New York who was doing the fitness inspiration with his friend? He was like 6 or 7 and he had this statement that he used to say when encouraging his friend, **"Strength no weakness!"**

This stuck with me for a while because he was telling his friend to keep at it, to keep strong, to keep working and to not leave any room for weakness to sink in and stop you from achieving what you are called to achieve. This aspect of character that we are going to be looking at next is steadfastness, and I thought there could be no better title for this chapter.

Many men in this generation are not leaders, they are followers who are led by culture, community, and social constructs. We allow others to dictate our decisions, but it's a paradox because when asked we say, **"I'm my own man I make my own decisions!"** But in reality, we are looking to our friendship group, society, social media for the validation of our decisions and our lives. This is one of the reasons why many men don't have good character; we're not steadfast. There are too many of us who forsake wise choices for popular choices, and this causes us to lack steadfastness.

You may have heard the statement before from parents on TV, **"If your friends jumped off of a cliff, would you do it too?"** This is a pivotal question and even though it seems farfetched; the principle still holds true. The principle is teaching us steadfastness; "Are you actually willing to relinquish your choice to someone else?" Because essentially what you're doing when you allow yourself to follow what everyone else is doing is, you're relinquishing your choice. As a man of God, you're only called to follow God and not your peers, and it's going to be tough because you may not be popular. You should be looking to stick with the only person who doesn't change and that's God! Be strong enough to say no to other opinions and culture! We are

WHAT IS A MAN?

called as men of God to do two things; be countercultural and to create a new culture for people to follow. If you're following the current culture, you're not doing your job as a man of God or a man of Character!

GOD WANTS US TO BE STEADFAST!

When we look at the scripture of Matthew 7:13-14 we get a clear directive from Jesus that as a man of character we are called to be steadfast and make wise choices! Don't pick the option that you see everyone going through, pick the right option, the God option, the one that is wise! We value numbers too much in this society, like we associate numbers with wisdom, the sort of **"If everyone is doing it then it must be right!"** We need to learn as men of God and character, to separate ourselves from the crowd.

DEFINING STEADFASTNESS

- Loyal
- Faithful
- Committed
- Devoted
- Dedicated
- Dependable
- Standing firm

A MAN OF CHARACTER IS A MAN WHO IS STEADFAST!

""Enter through the narrow gate. For wide is the gate and broad is the road that leads to destruction, and many enter through it. But small is the gate and narrow the road that leads to life, and only a few find it." Matthew 7:13-14 NIV

WHAT IS A MAN?

From this scripture there are two things we need to understand:

1. Easy doesn't mean right!

We see Jesus get quite commanding here as if He is dealing with a spirit that needs to be broken, He isn't asking a question or suggesting, He is just being honest! He is telling us the truth, the wide gate or the way of the world is going to be easier. It is easier to follow what everyone else is doing because you don't have to worry about clashing with anyone's perspective or habits.

Men of character don't choose the easy gate because they understand that accessibility, attraction, and prevalence do not determine validity or credibility. They understand that the easy option isn't always the right option, just because it takes less effort, appeals to our humanity or can make you popular, doesn't mean it is the right way.

Jesus even tells us something so key; ***"For wide is the gate and broad is the road that leads to destruction,"***

Jesus literally gives us the answers, but the problem is that we aren't used to picking the option that is tougher. Everybody wants the easy route, the clout and instant success. This spans across many areas of life as well as men, our character is deficient because we want instantaneous success, we want temporary pleasure because it looks good right then, but we don't understand that immediate pleasure isn't an indicator of it being right, hence why Jesus comes on so strong with these truths about the broad road. Yes, it may look appealing, but I want to let you know that it only leads to destruction, failure, and death. Are you going to choose death knowingly?

I believe personally that many of us have been so consumed with things being the easy way or believing we have made our own decisions, that we ignore the truth which is that these decisions kill us and our character! As men, we love shortcuts, getting

WHAT IS A MAN?

things for free, not having to earn things, and things that require minimum effort and maximum reward. This causes us to walk in the opposite nature to that of a man of Character.

Our desire to get things for free, reminds me of a TV programme my dad introduced our family too, which perfectly lays out how the enemy operates with the world and gives us a picture of how these people who walk through the wide gate end up fulfilling scripture. The show is called Hustle and is based in the UK with a team of con men and women who specifically go after people who *"Want something for nothing so they can give them nothing for something!"* These people are usually rich and lack character but they want more, as easy as they possibly can get it. These con men give them the appearance of a better life or further success; only for the mark (person who is being conned) to find out that this opportunity, open door, investment is what leads them to their death. Many of the people believe that everyone would do this, and this is one of the reasons why they end up losing everything.

A lot of us are like these people; we want things for free, so we choose the wide gate, and that gate is full of people like that. They want heaven without Jesus, millions without work, purity without sacrifice but what Jesus is doing here is He's letting you know, that although these may seem like appealing things, they aren't realistic, and you need to know the truth about pursuing the broad road. Jesus wants you to know the choice you are making when you decide to go down the broad road.

ARE YOU STEADFAST OR ARE YOU LOOKING FOR THE EASY LIFE?

WHAT IS A MAN?

2. Building a Steadfast Character

Someone who is steadfast makes wise choices, this is what is shown in the second verse of the passage. You aren't just born steadfast, this must be built, and it also has to be a continuous choice, when you give your life to Christ you have chosen to be steadfast, but you also have to make the choice every day, in every situation to affirm and confirm that choice.

Every time you choose to ignore the easy way, every time you endure things that come with standing out, every time you choose to sacrifice comfort to gain life you are being steadfast. Sometimes when we walk out life, we don't know why we are doing things or what the outcome will be, but God gives us a promise of how our character of steadfastness will result in life. This should be encouragement for all of us that if we just stay strong in times of trouble, if we just stay loyal to the Word of God then we have an eternal promise of life.

The easy way gives you the illusion that life is easy, that the way everyone is going is the right way just like the show Hustle. Jesus is saying if you are committed, if you're willing to make wise choices, if you're willing to forsake the opinions of man, if you're willing to be looked at funny for your choices then you will gain something that cannot be compared.

What I love about the Word is that Jesus lets us know this isn't easy, the narrow gate is narrow because not many people bother but also because there may be some things that need to be released from you when you go through the gate. What if you had to leave pride behind you to fit through the narrow gate? What if you had to release patience? What if you had to leave insecurity? What if you had to leave affirmation addiction?

Many of the things that you can carry through the wide gate are not going to fit when being steadfast! **They are not welcome in the narrow gate!** Hebrews talks about stripping off weight that

WHAT IS A MAN?

hold you down, and I think there can be weights that hold you from being steadfast which include things like affirmation addiction, insecurity, pride, impatience.

CHOOSE TO STRIP THE WEIGHTS OFF AND BE STEADFAST!

"Therefore, since we are surrounded by such a great cloud of witnesses, let us throw off everything that hinders and the sin that so easily entangles. And let us run with perseverance the race marked out for us," Hebrews 12:1 NIV

MAKE IT PRACTICAL

Now we know all about being steadfast, it is important to get some practical examples of how this will look in your life:

- Waking up early to read the Word instead of checking social media
- Abstaining from masturbation instead of giving yourself the excuse that it isn't sex
- Making sure you don't swear even if it isn't going to kill you
- Doing the work to prepare for exams instead of cheating
- Spending time in prayer and in the Word instead of watching movies
- Being honest and accountable about your struggles instead of hiding them
- Inviting people to church or bible studies instead of allowing them to always invite you to parties

We have to understand steadfastness in a practical way every day in our lives. If you know how to be steadfast then you will be in a better position to reflect the character of God! Every day we have the options to make wise choices that take us towards the narrow gate.

One thing we must understand is that just because we know the decisions to make, doesn't mean we're a committed to them. It is

WHAT IS A MAN?

important that you know the value of wise choices, think with foresight, and think with purpose.

RECAP

- God wants us to be steadfast
- Choose to strip off the weights that hold you down and be steadfast
- A man of Character is a man who is steadfast
- Stay committed to God, stay loyal to the Word
- Don't look for the easy
- Steadfastness is a daily commitment to life, to the Word and to wise choices.

WHAT IS A MAN?

Space for reflection

When reading this chapter and reviewing your life is there anything that you have noticed that stands out to you? Is there anything that has helped answer any questions you had about manhood? Use the space below to note anything down that you need to.

WHAT IS A MAN?

ACTION MAN

We have finally reached the end of our insight into character and we need to establish that the character keys are great, but the only way they are made manifest is through one's actions. Many of us have heard the phrase **"Actions speak louder than words"** and this is so true, many people can talk a good game but have no real substance or character. What we want to do is to learn how to be a man of character in its entirety. Be a man whose character is magnified and exemplified through his actions!

A MAN OF CHARACTER IS A MAN OF ACTION!

Jesus is telling us in Matthew 7:15-27 to not be prophets, disciples and builders who do not act the same way they speak; our actions need to reflect our character. He gives us an insight into why our actions are important, especially as men of God because we are looked to as an example, almost as pillars and reference points in this world and in our faith. We may be the only Jesus that someone sees, so our actions should reflect Him!

1. **Fruits reveal Roots**

""Watch out for false prophets. They come to you in sheep's clothing, but inwardly they are ferocious wolves. By their fruit you will recognize them. Do people pick grapes from thornbushes, or figs from thistles? Likewise, every good tree bears good fruit, but a bad tree bears bad fruit. A good tree cannot bear bad fruit, and a bad tree cannot bear good fruit. Every tree that does not bear good fruit is cut down and thrown into the fire. Thus, by their fruit you will recognize them." Matthew 7:15-20 NIV

Many unbelievers have a huge bone to pick with believers because of their actions; we seem to be the actions police when it comes to others, but we don't want to be held accountable when it comes to ourselves. They've seen pastors talk about sin

WHAT IS A MAN?

and then be caught cheating on their wife or they've seen Christians talk about being holy and then they're in the same clubs as them. We must make sure we watch out for this as believers, this isn't being a man of action!

We need to correct the discrepancy between what we are supposed to do and what we actually do. Why is it so easy for men of God to display different actions to that of what is expected of them? This is usually because their roots are not solid. They are not based on the Word; they are just like those of unbelievers but with the knowledge of the Word and what it expects.

We have gotten away with being hypocrites and not displaying the actions a man of God is supposed to for way too long, but this book is here to challenge those thoughts and break those habits. As men we have appeared to be righteous, but things aren't always as they seem. Our fruit will be tested and analysed, and we have to come through that because a man of God doesn't behave like a man of the world!

How do I know that you're a believer? Are your actions distinguished enough? Your character is made manifest through your actions. Do you look like a man of character based on your actions? Are you set apart by the way that you act? When will the time come when believers are noticed and set apart by its actions? Do you want to be the type of man who cannot be recognised as a man of God? Your roots should be God, His Word and looking like Him. Jesus was able to bear Good fruit because His root was God, and His Word. This needs to be the same for us, a relationship with the Holy Spirit and a knowledge of God's Word and the fruits of the spirit can cause us to walk out the actions we need to.

YOU CAN'T HAVE GOOD ROOTS AND PRODUCE BAD FRUIT!

WHAT IS A MAN?

2. Disciples have Directed Actions

""Not everyone who says to me, 'Lord, Lord,' will enter the kingdom of heaven, but only the one who does the will of my Father who is in heaven. Many will say to me on that day, 'Lord, Lord, did we not prophesy in your name and in your name drive out demons and, in your name, perform many miracles?' Then I will tell them plainly, 'I never knew you. Away from me, you evildoers!'" Matthew 7:21-23 NIV

Actions are so important as a man of character and it is especially important that your actions align with your words. We have heard the statement; **"Practice what you preach!"** but how many of us have looked at it, analysed it and assessed ourselves by it? Jesus describes in this scripture how, many of us will be coming to God on judgement day presenting a case for all the things we have done for Him and God won't care because He wants to know us and through all of zeal did you get direction for your actions? Men of character don't just act; they get direction so that they can **ACT RIGHT**!

Many of us are trying to convince people to have a relationship with God when we don't have one. Have you ever come across those people that are all about trying to get you involved in something but when you really check it out, they aren't really that sold out on it themselves? **All talk and no substance!**

Could it be that people aren't getting saved through you because they see you every day? Could it be that they see your actions and you don't look any different to them? You don't look like you're being directed by God! You don't look like the righteous who's steps are ordered by God! Therefore, it is important to be directed by God because your actions no longer come from a place of insecurity, but they come from a place of righteousness. Let's be real, because you don't have a solid enough relationship with God that it is causing you to live different, they don't want to join what you're offering them. They don't want God because you

WHAT IS A MAN?

don't look like your actions are set apart. But your actions aren't set apart because they're not directed by God!

We should also look at these verses as an extension of the previous passage; because you cannot call yourself a disciple of God if your actions don't come from the right place. Many of us do good things from the wrong place and wonder why we would be in this situation Jesus is describing here. Something that we need to understand is that false disciples act on behalf of God, but true disciples act with God and He works through them! If your steps are supposed to be ordered by God you need God to act, your character without God is nothing!

For those of you who have been working alone, all those actions you have been doing on behalf of God, using His name for things, this doesn't guarantee that you know God or that He is pleased. Your character doesn't become Godly by just doing God's work but by doing what He has called you to do; notice there's a difference. Doing God's work can be outside of your purpose or your current instructions but doing what God has called you to do means your steps are being ordered and you are following God's plan for you. Yes, it is important to be a man of actions but even more important you must have actions that have a basis and the premise of God! Disciples of God are directed by Him, they are only looking to act on and in the will of God.

IF YOUR ACTIONS AREN'T COMING FROM GOD THEN THEY AREN'T THE RIGHT ONES!

3. Build from a Strong Foundation!

""Therefore, everyone who hears these words of mine and puts them into practice is like a wise man who built his house on the rock. The rain came down, the streams rose, and the winds blew and beat against that house; yet it did not fall, because it had its foundation on the rock. But everyone who hears these words of mine and does not put them into practice is like a

WHAT IS A MAN?

foolish man who built his house on sand. The rain came down, the streams rose, and the winds blew and beat against that house, and it fell with a great crash." Matthew 7:24-27 NIV

God wants to prepare you to act right in life, He wants you to reflect Him; but to do this you need to build from the right foundation, you need to have character, humility, and wisdom! Don't just hear what the Word says but act on it; listen to the wisdom of God, listen to the Holy Spirit, discern what to do and what not to do, and **DO IT**!

Looking at this in context, I have an amazing example of building from a strong foundation for you: many of us, especially us as men, when we get a new gadget, bike, or piece of equipment around the house, we put it together without understanding the instructions in the manual. Most of the time we just like to get to work and then we wonder why we end up making mistakes when building. The person who built on sand just wanted to go with the flow, they didn't take any regard for if the foundation was strong enough or not.

HUMBLE YOURSELF AND READ THE MANUAL!

Make sure you read the manual and listen to the instructions so you can build something strong. What does that foundation look like in real life? It looks like Jesus and what you have learned from the Word, and that puts you in a great position to overcome because no matter what issues come your way your actions will hold up.

If you act from the right foundation, then your character will stand the test of turbulence. It is important for us to assess the foundation of our actions; a lot of us are acting from a place of pride, ignorance, inadequacy, or ignorance.

What sort of man are you? Do you act from a place that won't last or do you act from a place off the Word as a foundation?

WHAT IS A MAN?

YOUR WISDOM IS DEFINED BY YOUR ABLITY TO USE THE FOUNDATION OF CHRIST AS A PLATFORM FOR YOUR ACTIONS!

HOW TO ACT RIGHT

a) **What Fruits should I bear (Gal 5:22-23):**

"But the fruit of the Spirit is love, joy, peace, forbearance, kindness, goodness, faithfulness, gentleness and self-control. Against such things there is no law."

If your actions are centred around the fruits of the spirit then you are going to be reflecting the Holy Spirit and God in your actions. These are the sorts of attributes that you need to be showing every day, along with the other character keys we studied earlier in this section.

b) **What should drive my actions (Luke 2:49):**

"And He said to them, "Why did you seek Me? Did you not know that I must be about My Father's business?"

Make sure that God is the person leading and driving your actions. There is nothing worse than acting on behalf of God but not under the instruction of God and then He is displeased with you. Develop and cultivate the sort of relationship with God where your moves are inspired by Him and you begin to act from Him rather than from your assumption of Him. God knows the beginning and the end, so it also saves you time, heartache, and trials!

WHAT IS A MAN?

c) What foundation shall I build from (Josh 1:8):

"Be strong and very courageous. Be careful to obey all the law my servant Moses gave you; do not turn from it to the right or to the left, that you may be successful wherever you go. Keep this Book of the Law always on your lips; meditate on it day and night, so that you may be careful to do everything written in it. Then you will be prosperous and successful. Have I not commanded you? Be strong and courageous. Do not be afraid; do not be discouraged, for the Lord your God will be with you wherever you go."

Make sure that the foundation you are acting from is sure, solid and secure so that when tests and challenges come at you, you are secure and this can only happen if your character is informed by God! Spend time building yourself with the Word, understand the Word, meditating on it because what you meditate on will manifest. It is not enough to know the way you should act, you need to act that way, and the best foundation to do that from is Jesus, because it is solid, unchanging and can keep you.

RECAP

- Your actions are the final frontier of your character; they project everything that's going on the inside
- Many unbelievers are not becoming believers because we as believers don't act right
- Acting right is essentially acting in alignment with the will and Word of God
- Let your actions be led by God and Godly wisdom
- Talk less and do more, character is expressed through action!

WHAT IS A MAN?

Space for reflection

When reading this chapter and reviewing your life is there anything that you have noticed that stands out to you? Is there anything that has helped answer any questions you had about manhood? Use the space below to note anything down that you need to.

WHAT IS A MAN?

Myth #4: MEN ARE HARD

This myth is a big bug bear of mine! This whole, *"false strength, you have to be hard to be a man"* thing is a load of trash. This is a sign of insecurity in many men and in society that has created this false persona for men to follow. Allegedly a real man is tough as nails, strong as an ox and anything different isn't a real man.

The context of this myth is what takes it away from the truth; yes, men are supposed to be hard because we are supposed to be durable, solid, firm and not easily broken or bent, but we know this isn't the connotation society has for it. Society means superficial hardness which has nothing to do with being not easily broken, in will or ethics but instead means you can win a fight.

The biggest reason why this is a myth is because we believe that physical strength denotes complete strength; when it is only a facet, but also on top of that we must understand that strength comes from God and this myth brings into play an element of pride because it assumes the more you pump weights the harder you will be, WRONG, WRONG, WRONG!

""The Lord is my strength and my defence; he has become my salvation. He is my God, and I will praise him, my father's God, and I will exalt him." Exodus 15:2 NIV

SECTION 6: THE ROLE CALL

WHAT IS A MAN?

INTRODUCTION

Welcome to the Role Call! We are now going to take a look at the roles a man plays in life! This in-depth insight and analysis will help us to gain more understanding as to what the bible calls us to do in each of these roles, and how we should behave.

There are also some transferrable skills that should be used across every one of the roles. The role doesn't define you but everything we've learned so far defines who you are in the role and how you perform the role! God wants you to be the best man you can; this means you have to know what the biblical requirements or roles are for a man!

Many of us have struggled because we haven't understood that different roles play more of a priority in different seasons and knowing this can distinguish a boy from a man. There is an order and a protocol that isn't based upon age but based upon stage. When we look at the order that the roles are in, it gives us an insight into how God thinks and how He is a god of processes. There are things that need to be learned as a son that help you as a father, there are things you're called to do as a friend that prepare you well to be a better husband.

If you don't value the skills and lessons that you gain in each season, you are going to struggle because each role has a reason, and its priority has a season. Some of us are trying to focus on being a father before our time, some of us want to be a husband before our time but we haven't yet learned how to be a son or a friend. What do you have to teach your children? How can you be a role model of a man to your son if you aren't a son to your father?

What we have to realise is that God isn't silly, He doesn't want us to be learning on the job in the hardest relationships and roles we will play. This is why He allows us to experience microcosms of those relationships and roles earlier in our life. This is to teach us

WHAT IS A MAN?

the keys and important principles that are needed for life and the roles we will later play. Why do you think it is that is important to be able to have platonic relationships with women as a friend before you get into relationships? There are things you learn that are not isolated to that relationship but need carrying through into other relationships.

My prayer is that this chapter really changes your paradigm of the roles men play and gives you the keys necessary to become a better man. Some of you may not be playing some of the roles yet, so it is easier for you because you can get a head start and begin to learn in advance. However some of you are going to be challenged, so it is important that you are receptive and ready to grow. This is not my opinion and this is not to condemn you, but it is to give you God's Word on what you're called to do as a man, so that you have something to measure yourself by and apply every day.

It is important that we understand also what these different roles are that you will play:

1. A Son
2. A Brother
3. A Friend
4. A Husband
5. A Father

If you notice there is an order to this; when you leave the womb you become a son of your parents but then further down the line you become someone's husband and then someone's father.

If you see here, these are numbered, and they are in order! This is the biblical process of the stages a man goes through! These shouldn't be taken for granted or misplaced. Some of these roles you may not play due to your choice or even your parents' choice, but it is important for you to understand what you're called to do in each role!

WHAT IS A MAN?

Notice that in the biblical process you aren't called to be a father before you are a husband; this isn't because it doesn't happen in life but because you are called to grow and build in the correct stages. God is a god of covenant and you're not called to a role of such depth without covenant! If you have been there or currently are there, it isn't a problem because what is done is done. You can learn and still make choices in the future that help you to walk in your call for each role in life.

We see God in every single one of the roles because we are a reflection of God and His characteristics! Here are some examples that we can look at generically before we go into more detail for each role throughout this chapter:

A **son** must be disciplined, wise and obedient
A **friend** must be committed, helpful
A **brother** must be sacrificial, protective, an intercessor
A **husband** must be compassionate, protective, and walk in love
A **father** must comfort, lead, protect and provide

Let's begin this journey of discovering the callings that are associated with the roles of a man of God!

WHAT IS A MAN?

YO, SON

The first order of business when looking at the roles a man plays in life is to look at being a Son. We look at this first because the second you leave the womb and enter the earth you are someone's son. This is the foundation of your roles because you are a son of not just your earthly parents but God in heaven. The foundations you set in place from these relationships can inform the way you operate in the other roles you play in life. If you don't know how to be a son how do you set your future sons' standards? How can you be a role model to your sons if you haven't cultivated a relationship with God that would reflect the right character?

Not only is being a son a role but it is a calling, a mantle or even a responsibility. When you look at this, don't think of it as pressure but instead see it as a privilege. I believe that us as men don't perform the role of being a son well enough because we don't know how, we don't know what is required of us and we don't know God's opinion or wisdom on it.

What we are going to look at is what God calls sons to do and the best picture of that is **Jesus**! Jesus even in His divinity and superiority was still submitted to being a son! So, for you as a man not only are you the son of God but you are a son of Man.

Let's begin to look at some of the things that God calls a son to do or be:

WHAT IS A MAN?

HONOUR ROLL

We start here with honour! I believe this is where it starts, because honour oozes other actions and leads to a certain posture that God would want you to walk with. But what does this word mean? In Hebrew, the word honour means ***"Kabod"*** which means to give weight to someone. You have to understand how powerful you are as a son if you are called to honour.

I read in a leadership book that a leader is only affirmed as a leader if they have followers, so the power really lies with the followers. Just the same as with the son here; you bringing honour to your parents is what carries weight in their parenting. If you don't honour them, they are not affirmed in their parenthood.

"Children, obey your parents in the Lord, for this is right. "Honour your father and mother"—which is the first commandment with a promise— "so that it may go well with you and that you may enjoy long life on the earth." Ephesians 6:1-3 NIV

We need to understand that there are components to honour, like we can make honour practical to us and learn how to honour. The reason why many of you didn't honour your parents is because you didn't know what honour was. You didn't know how to measure it, what it looked like, and you didn't know it was a calling from God as a son. You may have heard the scripture, but have you understood it?

Honour is the foundation on which the rest of your callings as a son stand on. If there's no honour there's nothing. You are called to honour, and honour is the first commandment in the Bible with a promise, and that promise is long life! Now who wants long life? I mean I sure do… so let's look into the intricacies of honour!

WHAT IS A MAN?

"Honour is a gift that you give freely." Craig Groeschel

HOW TO HONOUR

The first thing we look at is **humility**. It takes humility to honour regardless of what you see or feel. Many of us in this current generation are led by our feelings and when it comes to honouring our parents sometimes, we might not feel like it, but this is why humility is the foundation of honour. If you aren't humble, you won't honour because you'll think about being right more than you will think about being humble. Sometimes when we look at humility, we have to prioritise and think about it relating to our parents from the perspective of prayer. The Word says that prayer is the highest form of humility; as a son, take your time to pray for your parents and even pray with them because this shows honour!

"if my people, who are called by my name, will humble themselves and pray and seek my face and turn from their wicked ways, then I will hear from heaven, and I will forgive their sin and will heal their land." 2 Chronicles 7:14 NIV

We then have to look at something that may be considered a swear word to some people... which is **obedience**! As a son obedience is key, because it is a necessary characteristic to have to display honour. In order to honour, you must obey. Obeying your parents in the Lord is key when displaying honour, not only because you are listening to what they are saying but through your obedience you are honouring their wisdom and their instruction!

"Children, obey your parents in the Lord, for this is right." Ephesians 6:1 NIV

It is important that your honour for your parents is shown through their **notability** in your life. Do you put your parents in a place of esteem and give them their place of importance in your

WHAT IS A MAN?

life? It is imperative to ensure because parents are uplifted, revered and treated as the Kings and Queens that they are in your life. You must treat your parents like they are important because that's what you are called to do; whether it's by the way you speak, the way you act or just your thoughts towards them. You have a responsibility to validate their worth with your actions; telling them you love them, getting them gifts and asking for their advice.

Sons are called to walk in **order**! In lifestyle, mindset and everything about you, you are not being asked but instead you are ordered to honour. When you look at a Prince, they have no choice but to honour because of who they are, this is the same as us. If you understand that you are an heir, then you begin to operate differently towards your parents. Your honour is also a reflection of who you believe you are. As a prince or future king, you walk in honour as a lifestyle because you realise that the father before you has paved the way for you to become who you are. Know your rights, know your inheritance, know what you possess, and your honour should be a result of this!

"Now if we are children, then we are heirs—heirs of God and co-heirs with Christ, if indeed we share in his sufferings in order that we may also share in his glory." Romans 8:17 NIV

You are called to live an **upright** life as a son! Your role is to display and reflect your family in everything you do; this is a decision as much as it is a calling. This is not something that you need divine intervention for, but it's something that you need the wisdom of God to be able to carry out every day. In order to live an upright life, you need to walk in wisdom which is also a calling of a son. We know that proverbs is full of scriptures to do with wisdom but there is one scripture in particular that shows us as sons, how living upright is wise and shows you're a gift to your parents. This is the call of God as a son behaves in honour. The mentality needs to be ***"I make the wise choices every day to live***

WHAT IS A MAN?

right because I am called to be a gift to my parents, and I want to bring them joy!"

"A wise son brings joy to his father, but a foolish man despises his mother." Proverbs 15:20 NIV

The final aspect of the honour roll is **respect**! Your life and your actions should come from a place of respect, if you don't respect your parents then you will never grow. Many of us are limited in our actions because we don't respect the source of them; we don't have enough respect for our parents to listen to what they say and actually put it into practice. Do you value the information you're being given? Most people are willing to listen to wisdom but the respect level they have for the giver of information determines their likelihood of actually implementing this information. You are called to respect your parents because this causes you to be a **doer** who not only hears their wisdom but actually does it. Do you respect your parents enough to listen to their wisdom or instruction and act upon it? That is something for you to think about. As sons we're called to move from the foundation of instruction, but we can't do that if we don't honour the instruction giver!

""Therefore, everyone who hears these words of mine and puts them into practice is like a wise man who built his house on the rock. The rain came down, the streams rose, and the winds blew and beat against that house; yet it did not fall, because it had its foundation on the rock." Matthew 7:24-25 NIV

HONOUR IS NOT ONLY A CALL BUT IT IS A CHOICE!

The emphasis of being a son is to walk in and walk out honour. You can't call yourself a son if you don't walk in any of these things, but the most important thing to understand is that the power is in your hands. No one can force you to honour your parents and that is why this is the staple of callings for a son; you are called to honour and if you understand what honour

WHAT IS A MAN?

entails you know that this is something that needs to be chosen and worked on intentionally!

Jesus was the perfect example of this, and it is funny that He did every single one of these things not only for His earthly parents but for God as well. He made it a life mission of His to honour God and His will/ purpose for His life. Now it's time for you to decide... Do I really want to walk in honour? I can't say that I honour God if I don't honour my parents so if I've been just honouring God and disregarding my parents, I need to check myself. Assess yourself and see if this is something that you may have been doing and then repent and change now that you have the wisdom.

"I have no greater joy than to hear that my children are walking in the truth." 3 John 1:4 NIV

RECAP

- Honour is the key heart posture needed to walk in the role of a son effectively
- You are called to honour but it's your choice whether you walk it out or not
- There's more to honour than just the dictionary definition
- Willingly choose to the honour your parents as you choose to honour God
- Honour is really a lifestyle not a one-time action!

WHAT IS A MAN?

Space for reflection

When reading this chapter and reviewing your life is there anything that you have noticed that stands out to you? Is there anything that has helped answer any questions you had about manhood? Use the space below to note anything down that you need to...

WHAT IS A MAN?

WASSUP BRUH

The next role that is going to be played by any man in their life is the role of a brother! Whether you're an older brother, adopted brother or a younger brother you have a responsibility and a call from God. Many of us don't have blood brothers but you may have come across someone in your life who becomes a brother to you or that you have become that brother for! When we study these roles it is not only to make you a better version of this person, but also for you to be able to assess those who hold those roles in your life. Whether your brother, your friend, or your father, this enables us to be able to have a standard of what to expect from them.

The role of a brother is not a joke at all, it is not something to be abused and not something to be neglected but it is a privilege. Many of us haven't had the greatest examples of brothers in our lives or even haven't had any but that shouldn't stop you from being a great brother to your siblings. We know that the fruits of the spirit are the basics of every single role that we play in life because they are the basics of life as a believer, but what we're looking at today are the calls of any brother!

BROTHER'S KEEPER

"Then the Lord said to Cain, "Where is your brother Abel?" "I don't know," he replied. "Am I my brother's keeper?" The Lord said, "What have you done? Listen! Your brother's blood cries out to me from the ground." Genesis 4:9-10 NIV

We are called to be our brother's keeper and before we delve into this it is important for us to understand what this means;

"a keeper is one who has the care, custody, or superintendence of anything."

WHAT IS A MAN?

As you can see in the story of Cain and Abel this is the first example of brotherhood in the Word and we see a big problem that occurs because Cain after killing Abel asks God a strong question; *"Is it my job to look after and protect my brother?"* God's response to this question is so profound and I wanted to make sure that it is addressed and understood. In the question that Cain asked, he opened up a room for a teaching moment. He opened a conversation for what we should and shouldn't expect from our brothers. He gave us perspective!

Many of us may believe that it is self-explanatory to not kill your brother but if you're not being your brother's keeper, then you are still killing your brother you're just not doing it physically. Cain sets us on a journey to discover what a brother is called to do as part of being the **brother's keeper!**

a) Unity in Doing God's Will

"How could one man chase a thousand, or two put ten thousand to flight, unless their Rock had sold them, unless the Lord had given them up?" Deuteronomy 32:30 NIV

One of the most important callings of a brother is to bring unity through doing Gods will; something we see from Cain is that he and Abel were both unified in bringing offerings. Cain was more interested in the competition between him and his brother rather than doing the will of God, hence why instead of learning the lesson of sowing and giving offerings he killed his brother. Cain saw his deficiency as a door for competition rather than an opportunity to learn and grow; he was jealous, angry, insecure, and that caused division between him and Abel which angered him so much he killed Abel.

Your sibling is not your competition, they're not the enemy, they're there for you to love, protect, keep, and to steward! Steward their life, their heart, and build their relationship with God.

WHAT IS A MAN?

Are you helping them grow or helping them to die with your words, your actions, your heart?

- How do you speak to your siblings?
- What is your mentality towards your siblings?
- Do you care about your sibling's safety?
- How important are your siblings to you?
- Are you trying to grow your relationship with your siblings?
- How often do you check on your sibling's mental health?
- Do you know the things that your siblings care about?
- Have you created a space of honesty and vulnerability for your siblings?

"Therefore, confess your sins to each other and pray for each other so that you may be healed. The prayer of a righteous person is powerful and effective." James 5:16 NIV

b) Righteous Influence

When you can begin to walk with your siblings in the will of God; uplifting them, praying for them, praying God's will over them then you are doing your role as a brother. You have a responsibility to push them to destiny by being united in God's will. Your role as a brother can be key in keeping your siblings in purpose and in the direction God wants them to go in. Not only are you supposed to be an influence on your siblings, but a righteous influence! You need to make sure your actions, lifestyle and communication are righteous!

BE RIGHTEOUS IN LIVING SO YOU CAN BE A RIGHTEOUS INFLUENCE!

Some believe that it's only important to be a righteous influence when you're an older sibling, but it is vital as a brother in general. As men we have a responsibility to be leaders, we have a responsibility to model what we want to see and to be the managers of relationships. We have to make sure we are living, breathing examples of the righteousness that we expect to see from our siblings.

We need to understand the gravity of the call, you have a responsibility to your siblings that you don't do anything that could lead them to sin. For some that may be as simple as the music you listen to; make sure that you're not listening to any music that could cause your siblings to sin. Don't watch movies that could cause them to sin, don't bring them to environments that could trigger things in them or bring up old struggles. This is your responsibility; you should be self-aware, constantly assessing and looking at your life and actions to see how this may affect your siblings. If you're not a righteous influence it is a sin according to God.

The life of Abel, even though short lived showed us a righteous influence but it wasn't responded to in the right way. Abel lived righteously and showed Cain through his offering what God expects from his children in terms of offerings. This is something you can take note of as a brother; if you can lead your siblings by a righteous example then it shows you're a brother!

I want you to be able to be a better brother, you can only do this by knowing the call, knowing what is required and knowing what it takes! With this information and the foundation of being your brother's keeper you are able to build on this and begin to walk out your call of being a brother!

You may not have been a great brother so far; you may not even be a brother but at least because of this information you can learn what is needed. This is not to judge you or tell you you're a bad brother but to give you the tools you need to be able to become who God has called you to be. This is something that you can look at for when looking at your brothers, is this the way they operate with you? You may even be a father or mother, who can use this information on how to help your sons to become better brothers.

WHAT IS A MAN?

RECAP

- You are called to be your brother's keeper
- You are called to be a righteous influence
- You are called to live a righteous life
- You are called to assess yourself, your actions, everything about you to ensure it doesn't negatively affect your siblings
- You have a responsibility to steward your siblings and their lives.

WHAT IS A MAN?

Space for reflection

When reading this chapter and reviewing your life is there anything that you have noticed that stands out to you? Is there anything that has helped answer any questions you had about manhood? Use the space below to note anything down that you need to...

WHAT IS A MAN?

NO NEW FRIENDS

This role is going to be so interesting because it is something that is so commonly misused and misconstrued that it has lost its meaning, its purpose and its weight! Nowadays you can meet someone and the next day you're friends; we have Facebook friends and Instagram friends, so we have this misconception about friends and their importance.

What really is a friend? What is the meaning and what are the callings associated with being a friend? The reason why we have such shallow and poor relationships is because we don't know the real answers to these questions. We aren't able to properly apply the principles of friendship because we don't know them. What we are going to go through is going to make you a better friend but also it is going to allow you to assess if you have been a true friend to those who call you a friend now.

A) DESTINY HELPER

**"As iron sharpens iron, so one person sharpens another."
Proverbs 27:17 NIV**

To sharpen:
- Make or become sharp or sharper
- To improve or cause to improve

Being a destiny helper is something that is key to a friend's development and growth in all of the areas of their life. You need to be willing to push them to purpose, to sharpen them up. In order to do this you have to be sharp yourself; which would require you as a friend to be on top of your game in life and walking in purpose, because you can't help a person to somewhere you've never been! Think about your life and your friendships; are you encouraging them, are you building them? Do you keep up to date with their progress in areas they are saying they want to go into whether business, career, or academics? Are you making them better? These are the sorts of questions you need to be asking yourself when it comes to friendship. A friend is supposed to sharpen their friend and that can be seen in many different areas, that could be via relationship with God, character, productivity, or in purpose. Whatever it is are you enhancing it? Ask yourself and assess honestly!

When we look at the definition of Iron it is "a strong hard magnetic metal which represents, Firmness, Strength & Resistance!" So, when we look at this from our perspective as a man, this should surely play into our bravado and masculine image that we have.

A real strong person doesn't expose somebody else's weakness but instead builds someone's strength. As a friend, if you are not iron yourself then it is going to be hard for you to sharpen your friend who is iron. You have to be firm with your friends, you have to be willing to tell them the truth, be willing to shut them up when their communication doesn't match their destiny, or you should be willing to resist anything that opposes their destiny. Are you willing to do these things?

How to help a friend's destiny:
- Care about their destiny
- Keep yourself sharp
- Encourage them
- Strengthen them
- Resist anything that can slow/ blunt them
- Have your focus as their improvement

WHAT IS A MAN?

B) CONFIDANT

"One who has unreliable friends soon comes to ruin, but there is a friend who sticks closer than a brother." Proverbs 18:24 NIV

A Confidant is "a person with whom one shares a secret or private matter, trusting them not to repeat it to others." Everybody needs a confidant in their life, because not only does it denote someone who feels safe with you but also someone that is able to entrust you with information that is important to them. This needs to be earned and gained especially in this day and age where you can pay to get information out of people, or you can just post it on social media anonymously and no one would know that you shared the secret. When we look at a friend, they should be close, someone you can share your life with, someone you can share secrets with and someone who you trust with God's visions and plans for your life.

As a friend there is a call to be a confidant. This may not be the case for all of the people you associate with but anyone that you consider a friend. If you're not willing to tell them secrets or they don't trust you with theirs then you're not friends. I believe the reason why this scripture mentions unreliable friends and the closer than a brother is because unreliable people cannot be trusted but the premise of your trust from a friend is through it being earned. A sibling doesn't have to earn your trust, you trust them because you're related by blood and assume that the blood is the key to them being trustworthy. News flash: **IT ISN'T**. With a friend you need to have proven your worth, they need to prove trustworthiness, there is nothing inside of you wanting to innately trust someone who isn't blood, so this has to be built.

You have to foster a level of trust with your friends where they trust you with their life, and then their information won't be a problem, and their burdens won't be a problem. You have to love them as you love yourself and ensure they know that. Check your

WHAT IS A MAN?

track record as a friend as you're reading this; what have you done with their information they've given you? Have you spilled their secrets? Have you held their secrets against them? Have you tried to sabotage them?

"And the second is like it: 'Love your neighbour as yourself.'" Matthew 22:39 NIV

It is important to be self-aware, ensure the **heart and safety** of your friend comes as a high priority to you.

Tips on being a confidant:
- You need to be available
- You need to be a listener
- You need to be a carer
- You need to create a space for them to be vulnerable
- You need to encourage openness
- You need to affirm them
- You have to reassure them

A CONFIDANT ENSURES THAT THEY KEEP THE CONFIDENCE OF THEIR FRIEND AT ALL TIMES!

C) CHARACTER BUILDER

"Do not be misled: "Bad company corrupts good character."" 1 Corinthians 15:33 NIV

Many of us as friends need to be held accountable biblically for our actions as friends. We have heard this scripture many times, but have we looked at it properly? Have we really looked at our influence on our friends? Have we studied what our role is and how we impact the character of our friends?

'Bad company corrupts good character' is such a powerful statement but I'm not sure if we assess ourselves by it properly and understand it. The key to this is that character is being

WHAT IS A MAN?

influenced by bad company. Many of us complain about the character of our friends, but could we be the reason why their character isn't where it is supposed to be? You need to check how you are as company!

As a friend you are supposed to build the character of someone, you are called to be good company! It is important to ascertain what company means and that is: 'being around someone, your friends, your circle, your people of influence'.

Here are some questions that you need to ask yourself that will help you to decide whether you are helping your friends' character or not:

- Are you leading them closer to Christ?
- Are you making them a better person?
- Are you challenging their morals in a positive way?
- Are you challenging their dysfunction?
- Are you holding them to a higher standard?
- Are you refining their speech?
- Are you correcting them?
- Are you helping them stay away from sin?

If you notice you're not being a good influence, then it is quite easy to repent and work on how you impact their lives. If you aren't willing to be a better influence, then you aren't a friend of theirs because friendship is a commitment and calling to building the character of an individual. No person should be your friend and stay the same or get worse in character and morals, so it means that you need to ensure that your character is right so that you're classed as good company. You have a responsibility to improve your friends, and to serve the person you have chosen as a friend by trying to better them!

WHAT IS A MAN?

RECAP

- Friendship is all about service
- You are called to improve your friends
- Your friend's future should be important to you, their life, their character, and their heart should be a priority
- In order to be a confidant, you need to be trustworthy and keep the confidence of your friend
- Friends have to be sharp as well, to make sure they can sharpen
- Sometimes you have to be firm with your friends to ensure that they grow

WHAT IS A MAN?

Space for reflection

When reading this chapter and reviewing your life is there anything that you have noticed that stands out to you? Is there anything that has helped answer any questions you had about manhood? Use the space below to note anything down that you need to...

WHAT IS A MAN?

ISSA HUSBAND

It is so interesting in this generation how much further backwards we have gone. In the past it used to be seen as a privilege to be a husband and spend the rest of your life with someone but over time we have reduced it to a name that comes after a piece of paper and an expensive wedding. The sacred nature has left, the honour, the covenant, and the joy of God's divine connection have gone also. Many become fathers before they become husbands, they become fathers and never become a husband and some people have no care for ever being a husband because they don't value its importance! In God's design, a man should be a husband before a father and there are some things that you are called to do and be as a husband!

**"Husbands love your wives, just as Christ loved the church and gave himself up for her to make her holy, cleansing her by the washing with water through the word, and to present her to himself as a radiant church, without stain orns are wrinkle or any other blemish, but holy and blameless. In this same way, husband's ought to love their wives as their own bodies. He who loves his wife loves himself. After all, no one ever hated their own body, but they feed and care for their body, just as Christ does the church— for we are members of his body. "For this reason, a man will leave his father and mother and be united to his wife, and the two will become one flesh.""
Ephesians 5:25-31 NIV**

The main thing you need to do as a husband is **Love** and this is expressed in many different ways! Let's begin to explore what this love means and looks like. Love must be the foundation and the motivation of everything you do as a husband, but not just any type of love. A man is called to love his wife as Christ loved the church so that's a whole new standard, it's like a deep sacrificial type of love.

WHAT IS A MAN?

We can see below Christ's love explained:

- Jesus died for the church
- Jesus built the foundations of the church
- Jesus was committed to the church
- Jesus was ridiculed for the church
- Jesus made the church holy
- Jesus valued the church as He valued His own life
- Jesus fed the church
- Jesus cared for the church
- Jesus led the church
- Jesus uplifted the church

What we see here is an introduction to being a husband, everything you do and are called to do is fuelled by love!

What to sacrifice?
- You need to sacrifice your time
- You need to watch the movies she likes
- You need to go shopping with her when you don't like shopping
- You need to listen to how her day went at work
- You need to be able to listen to her problems
- You need to prioritise her heart and her safety
- You need to sacrifice your opinion for the sake of the relationship
- You need to sacrifice time to pray for her and cover her
- You need to give her the attention she desires
- You need to be able to build her as well as building yourself
- You need to creatively think of ways to show your love and intentionality
- You need to sacrifice to provide and to protect
- You need to give up the single mentality
- You need to give up selfishness
- You need to give up personal agenda
- You need to give up the "me" mentality

WHAT IS A MAN?

A) Provide

"Anyone who does not provide for their relatives, and especially for their own household, has denied the faith and is worse than an unbeliever." 1 Timothy 5:8 NIV

This is one of the most controversial things we discuss in this generation, especially because of the new and dare I say advanced gender roles where men are not specifically assigned the role of provider anymore. What I love about the Bible is that it transcends culturally defined words, like provider. When we think provider we think money, but God wants you to know as a husband provision is way more than money and that's why you need to understand it as part of loving your wife!

Before you even get the opportunity to provide for a family you need to have put the things in place to provide for your wife. Do you have a plan to provide? Do you know what things you are called to provide a wife? Have you been walking in what God calls you to as a provider? The Word says, you are called to provide and that if you don't you are worse than an unbeliever. People probably didn't even know this scripture existed but just like this book the Word gives you the answers, so that you can properly prepare before marriage. If you haven't got these things sorted, then it's going to be a big problem. If you have no plan, you're not ready to be a husband! God takes your provision seriously hence why the statement is so drastic.

If you want to see an example of provision look at the feeding of the 5,000; Jesus started by providing the people with a **place** where they could learn and hear His words, then after that He provided them with the **information** that they came for but finally He provided something else, which was the **food** they needed to deal with their hunger because they had been there for a while. If you are going to have people around you, if you're going to be responsible for people, if you're going to steward people you

WHAT IS A MAN?

have to be providing them with something and we see from Jesus it isn't just money, you need to provide other things.

Provision is more than just finances, there are a number of things that need to be provided for your wife that have nothing to do with money:

- Can you provide leadership?
- Can you provide love?
- Can you provide protection?
- Can you provide safety?
- Can you provide direction?
- Can you provide results?

Provision is more than money but that doesn't discount the fact that a major problem many relationships have is the money problem.

B) Lead

"But if serving the Lord seems undesirable to you, then choose for yourselves this day whom you will serve, whether the gods your ancestors served beyond the Euphrates, or the gods of the Amorites, in whose land you are living. But as for me and my household, we will serve the Lord."" Joshua 24:15 NIV

Leadership is not about dictation but instead it is about service and sacrifice! Jesus shows us this throughout the Bible! Men are the managers of relationships and many of them instead of managing have been manipulating, so if you are learning to lead you are also learning to manage.

There is a phenomenal way that Jesus shows us how to lead as a husband and that is leading with love. A leader leads from the front in terms of going forward and going through the trials first but they are also behind to push you forward. A leader stands up for their followers and protects them; Jesus shows leadership as

WHAT IS A MAN?

being wise, having vision, having foresight, these things are all vital to a man for being a leader as a husband. Jesus shows us how to lead from the future, He leads based upon the future needing to come to pass in this time. You need a vision from God and then His direction because you cannot lead your wife if you aren't led by God!

You have a responsibility to get vision for your life, and your wife so that you're able to lead her correctly because God will give it to you!

As a leader here are some things that you need to get vision for:

- The vision for your partnership
- The vision for your purpose
- The vision for your future kids
- The vision for your family
- The vision for your exploits
- The vision for your location

LEAD YOUR WIFE WITH GOD AND BY LOVE!

C) Uplift

"Two are better than one, because they have a good return for their labor: If either of them falls down, one can help the other up. But pity anyone who falls and has no one to help them up. Also, if two lie down together, they will keep warm. But how can one keep warm alone?" Ecclesiastes 4:9-11 NIV

I may be crossing contemporary culture with this doctrinal look at being a husband, but this is vital! Many men are in marriages where they are competing with their wives to prove their masculinity and degrading their wives to make themselves feel more manly!

WHAT IS A MAN?

As a man of God, you are called to uplift your wife and I know this may seem like a foreign concept because many men believe that it's all about them, but relationships are two way and you have a responsibility to uplift your wife. You have to support her, not just financially but emotionally, spiritually, mentally and physically. She needs to know that you care enough to lift her mood. You need to establish your wife, push her to purpose and use your strength to uplift her and not to oppress her.

If you are going to be with a woman, then you have to be elevating her, take her to new levels in all areas of her life, help her overcome her insecurities, tell her she's beautiful, speak life over her and declare the Word over her! You as a man have a big responsibility to establish your wife, not just when married but before that you lift her from singleness to married life. You are not there to just draw from her but you're there to build her because the scripture talks about "two being better than one" which means there's something significant about you doing your job, if she's the only one giving, building, and establishing then it's a one-way marriage. This should be a collective but as a man you have to hold up your end and do something that may seem unnatural in culture for a man and uplift your wife.

When you do your job as a husband then there should be extra for your wife:

- Extra faith
- Extra prayer
- Extra strength
- Extra comfort
- Extra knowledge
- Extra wisdom
- Extra power

When you look back upon these things, are you doing any of these? Or as a man who's single how many of these make sense to you? Are you willing to do these things?

WHAT IS A MAN?

One of the greatest ways to uplift your wife is through prayer, lifting her up to God every day and looking for His insight on how to love her, lead her, build her and support her!

- Do You pray for her purpose?
- Do you pray for her peace?
- Do you pray for her wellbeing?
- Do you pray for her mental health?
- Do you pray for her spirit?
- Do you pray for her heart?

There are things on the inside of your wife that are waiting to be confirmed and affirmed by your voice but if you do not play your role, they may never be activated just like we see in Genesis 2 when Adam met Eve. His words activated her calling and her purpose as a woman but also her position in his life. This is the same for you as a husband!

BUILD HER FAITH, CONFIDENCE, STRENGTH AND COMPETENCE!

"The tongue has the power of life and death, and those who love it will eat its fruit." Proverbs 18:21 NIV

RECAP

- Being a godly husband is all about sacrifice
- Love is expressed in many different ways as a husband
- You're called to provide for your wife
- You're called to lead your wife
- You're called to uplift your wife
- Provision goes beyond money and into deeper things like support, love, leadership, time, and vision

WHAT IS A MAN?

Space for reflection

When reading this chapter and reviewing your life is there anything that you have noticed that stands out to you? Is there anything that has helped answer any questions you had about manhood? Use the space below to note anything down that you need to...

WHAT IS A MAN?

GOOD GOOD FATHER

Being a father is the height of the roles that you play as a man. You have to have gone through a serious process before you even get here. The role of a father is a big responsibility, but it is just a new level. If you look at the roles we have looked at so far, they all contain elements that have callings or skills that are transferable because God doesn't give you a new level with no foundation.

What we are going to see here is that there are elements of things from every other stage that you will be required or called to do. There is such a great calling and responsibility on being a father and it is a blessing because we have the perfect example in God. Notice how I didn't say your earthly father? That is because let's be honest it is not normal for fathers to play the role of a father perfectly in the world today.

Some young men haven't had a father, some have fathers who aren't playing their role, and some have fathers who do play their role. Young men are all in different places and scenarios when it comes to their home situation but something that can be guaranteed is that as a whole, men haven't been fathered very well.

Maybe some of the people reading this book may be women, who are looking at this to see what they need to see in a man who is going to be a father to her kids. These callings that have been given for a father are to help and measure where you are at as a man and help you in fulfilling your role.

You are not ready to be a father just because you have impregnated a woman, your child doesn't call you to be a father, a father is much more than having a kid, the ability to make children the ability to earn money, and tell people what to do, it goes deeper than that.

WHAT IS A MAN?

LOVE

The foundation of being a father is Love!

"So, he got up and went to his father. "But while he was still a long way off, his father saw him and was filled with compassion for him; he ran to his son, threw his arms around him and kissed him. "The son said to him, 'Father, I have sinned against heaven and against you. I am no longer worthy to be called your son.' "But the father said to his servants, 'Quick! Bring the best robe and put it on him. Put a ring on his finger and sandals on his feet. Bring the fattened calf and kill it. Let's have a feast and celebrate. For this son of mine was dead and is alive again; he was lost and is found.' So, they began to celebrate." Luke 15:20-24 NIV

The story of the son with prodigal living is about the son but it is also about the father. It is a perfect example of a love that surpasses everything you do, an unconditional love. This father shows a love that is more important than being right, one that covers a multitude of sins, cares for reconciliation, gives mercy, and that doesn't change its view of its child based on sin or wrongdoing.

This scripture is an example of how God fathers us and how fathers are supposed to father their children. Fathers must have a love that surpasses their preferences, that doesn't cut people off, or hold things against their kids and doesn't shun their kids for their decisions.

Something we have to understand is that the love of the father is there regardless of the actions of the child, so this will mean that ***"Disagreement and disobedience from a son doesn't lead to denial from the father"*** and ***"Repentance doesn't lead to restricted reconciliation!"*** We see this lived out in this scripture because the father received the son back to the full state that he left, he didn't change his perspective of his son, all he saw was

WHAT IS A MAN?

his son. This is the same as God when He sees us, all He sees is the ones He loves.

"Above all, love each other deeply, because love covers over a multitude of sins." 1 Peter 4:8 NIV

Are you willing to love your child beyond limits? Many times as your child grows, they are going to make their own decisions and potentially do things that you don't agree with but how do you respond to that? Something that is essential for a father to do is create spaces and environments for his children to live and operate in! You need to create an environment of love and safety, where they can come to you and feel as though they are able to share burdens with you. Therefore because of that space created they are more likely to live a life of honour because they don't want to disrespect the space you've created and abuse your love! You taking the time to create that space and constantly affirming it can determine the response and shape the mindset of your children!

a) COACH

"Start children off on the way they should go, and even when they are old, they will not turn from it." Proverbs 22:6 NIV

As the father in the house you are called to be the Head Coach, which means you're called to train your kids, to prepare them in the ways of God, to give them the wisdom and knowledge required to be successful believers in life, to assess them, to build them, encourage them, to develop them and nurture them. Your kids should consistently be growing under your coaching because a coach is judged on the performance and development of their players.

You must steward your kids and understand the responsibility you have to them, to make sure that they start off in the right way, to train them correctly. Just like football coaches, you

WHAT IS A MAN?

should know what the standard is so you are able to coach them to standard. We know the standard is the Word so if you don't know the Word you can't *train them in the way they should go!* You need to have a relationship with God and be hearing from God to father correctly. You should be constantly assessing yourself and your walk, causing you to be a living example to your kids of the way they should go!

A COACH IS AN EXAMPLE OF THE WISDOM THAT HE IS TEACHING!

"Whoever spares the rod hates their children, but the one who loves their children is careful to discipline them." Proverbs 13:24 NIV

With coaching also comes discipline, because the way you should go will take discipline but also coach's journey have to discipline anyone who goes against what the rules and codes of conduct are for the club or the team. So as a father if you don't discipline your kids, it means you don't care about their character long term and you don't love them. Bear in mind I'm not saying discipline is violence because discipline can take many forms, including teaching the right practices, repetition, correction.

We need to ensure that we don't westernise every word and vilify it. The importance of discipline is to be self-aware because some of the actions you may be seeing are a result of your actions. You need to focus on fixing your actions rather than disciplining your child for repeating them.

WHAT IS A MAN?

b) LEAVE AN INHERITANCE

"A good person leaves an inheritance for their children's children, but a sinner's wealth is stored up for the righteous." Proverbs 13:22 NIV

Many people are looking at this and they think it is just about finances and for the most part it is, but there is so much more to legacy and inheritance than money. If all you can provide or leave your kids is money, then you've only done part of your job. As a father your responsibility is not just to your kids but your legacy, you need to take care of your kid's kids.

If you're a father and you haven't thought about or haven't got an inheritance to leave then you need to make sure you read this and take actions from now to ensure that you put these things in place. If you're a husband now preparing to be a father, then you need to make sure you are looking at and assessing what will my future generations have to take from me? Think about what you have to offer them!

I want to help you by explaining to you some of the things that you can leave as an inheritance so that you have a measurement or some sort of direction because what God left for the world was way more than money; He left the Gospel, the Holy Spirit, love, the opportunity for a relationship with Him. As a father, God has left a legacy that we are still walking in now.

As a father, think about the inheritance you can leave:

- Wisdom
- Values & Standards
- Faith in Jesus
- Ministry
- Business
- Innovative ideas
- Gifts, Skills and Talents

WHAT IS A MAN?

Are you starting to see a picture of the inheritance you should be leaving for your children? This is a high priority for your life as a father because you want to be considered a good father by God's standards! Think trans-generationally with everything that you do! How does what I'm doing now affect my future?

c) COVER

"Very early in the morning, while it was still dark, Jesus got up, left the house and went off to a solitary place, where he prayed." Mark 1:35 NIV

As a father is the head of the house, he has the responsibility to cover his family. This scripture is so profound because what we see from Jesus even though we don't get complete detail into exactly what His prayer points were, we can see that He got up before everyone to pray. When I look at this, I see that Jesus was presenting His day to God and placing it in His hands, waiting for instructions. Whilst doing this He was also covering His disciples in prayer and everyone that He would come into contact with that day.

The definition of cover is:
- put something on top of or in front of (something), especially in order to protect or conceal it.
- shelter or protection sought by people in danger

This is what a father is supposed to do, you are supposed to be the spiritually covering for your house. You should rise up early to make sure you pray for and over your family. That means you need to be able to pray, to fight in the spirit realm for your family, and to declare things over your wife and kids.

As their covering you need to be able to receive a word of the Lord for them, receive direction concerning them, discern things in their life and to stand in front of them as their protection. This may sound like it's a tough ask, but it is important that as a man

WHAT IS A MAN?

you know exactly what you're called to do as a father before you choose to become one. You need to be prepared so you're able to assess where you are currently at and get more wisdom.

"Or again, how can anyone enter a strong man's house and carry off his possessions unless he first ties up the strong man? Then he can plunder his house." Matthew 12:29 NIV

You are the strong man of your house and many of us interpret this scripture as the family of the strong man can bind him causing them to be plundered but the perspective I want us to look at this scripture from, is that if you're not spiritually built up then you're not going to be able to protect your family. Many of us are getting built in the gym but we are spiritual twigs, we probably couldn't bench 10kg in the spirit. This is something that needs to get dealt with and understood; if you aren't built and strengthened in prayer you cannot protect your house or cover your children.

"For our struggle is not against flesh and blood, but against the rulers, against the authorities, against the powers of this dark world and against the spiritual forces of evil in the heavenly realms." Ephesians 6:12 NIV

Let us not become so obsessed with the title that we forget the responsibility, call and mandate. Your child is a seed and you need to cover your seed to ensure that it doesn't get spoiled by the enemy.

WHAT IS A MAN?

RECAP

- Fathers are called to love, which is expressed through coaching, leaving an inheritance, and covering
- Having a relationship with God is key to fatherhood
- If God isn't your father, you're not likely to reflect Him
- Leaving an inheritance goes deeper than money
- A coach is an example of the wisdom he is teaching

WHAT IS A MAN?

Space for reflection

When reading this chapter and reviewing your life is there anything that you have noticed that stands out to you? Is there anything that has helped answer any questions you had about manhood? Use the space below to note anything down that you need to...

WHAT IS A MAN?

Myth #5: ALL MEN ARE SPERM DONORS

This may seem like a crude statement, but it is something that we need to address in this world. *"Sperm donor v father"* this argument is a big one because many men seem to want to just make babies but not actually take care of them.

This is however a myth because not all men are like this, but we seem to be in a major crisis when it comes to fatherhood. We have many men who are leaving women alone to look after children and that is something that would cause a statement like this to seem true.

As a man I'm not sure what circumstances you would have to be in to leave your child, but a lot of it comes from the lack of responsibility among men and the diminishing of the importance of sex. When we don't value the sacred bond of sex, we begin to have situations like this. Many see it as just a sexual encounter but it is more than just that, it is the opportunity to father and bring life.

We need to understand the purpose of sex and the covenant that comes with it; this is the official seal of union and the spiritual connection that is not easily broken. We need to be sure that as well as this covenant it also comes with a responsibility to go beyond the fixation of pleasure and instead to manage the consequence of that sexual encounter which is a child.

"Children are a heritage from the Lord, offspring a reward from him." Psalms 127:3 NIV

WHAT IS A MAN?

Notes

Use the space below to note anything down that you need to, whether it be an action plan, stand out points or just any notes...

WHAT IS A MAN?

WHAT IS A MAN?